I0161102

Auntie's Voice

Copyright owned by
Cora E Wiltse.
2009
All rights reserved

Christian Poetry
PO Box 20009
Carson City Nevada 89721
thebettysbooks.com

The right of reproduction of this book is reserved exclusively for the author who grants permission for brief quotes to be used for review purposes as long as full credit is given to the author.

"Thou shalt not muzzle the ox that treadeth out the corn. And, the laborer is worthy of his reward." 1 Timothy 5:18 (1 Corinthians 9:9, Deuteronomy 25:4, Luke 10:7, Matthew 10:10, Deuteronomy 24:15.)

"Therefore, behold, I am against the prophets, saith the Lord, that steal my words every one from his neighbor." Jeremiah 23:30

...Thou shalt not steal, ... Thou shalt love thy neighbor as thyself." Romans 13:9 (Matthew 19:18, Mark 10:19, Luke 18:20, 1 Corinthians 6:8,10, Ephesians 4:28, Exodus 20:15, Leviticus 19:11,13, Deuteronomy 5:19, Leviticus 19:18, Matthew 5,:43, 7:12, 19:19, 22,:39, Mark 12:31, Luke 10:27, Galatians 5:14, James 2:8)

"Render therefore to all their dues: ... honor to whom honor." Romans 13:7

"That no man go beyond and defrauds his brother in any matter: because that the Lord is the avenger of all such, as we also have forewarned you and testified." 1 Thessalonians 4:6 (Leviticus 19:13, Deuteronomy 32:35, Proverbs 22:22, 23)

Scriptures compiled by the Bluedorns, Triviumpursuit.com.

Cover Picture by Auntie

Merriel Pauline English was born February 6, 1914 to Herbert and Effie English in Sedgwick Colorado. She was the fourth child, (their second daughter) out of thirteen, half of whom died in childhood. They traveled a great deal in her early years, including coming to California by covered wagon.

Merriel married Forest Haworth on September 5, 1935 in Ontario, California. They were never blessed with children of their own. However, Auntie, as most of us knew her, helped to raise many nieces and nephews. Forest passed away December 23, 1977, after 37 years of marriage. We lost our Auntie in January 18, 1999.

These are a collection of poems and original artwork found among her belongs after her death. She would be pleased for us all to enjoy them.

We have tried not to duplicate. If we did, please forgive us.

Betty Sue Tracy and Betty Wiltse

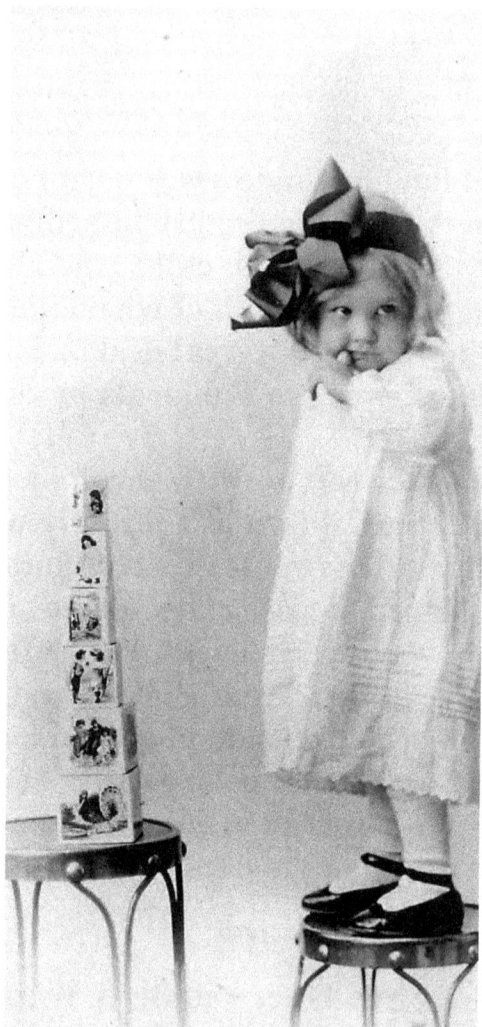

Merriel age 2

My Coming King
Jesus Christ my Savior
He means more to me than all worldly treasure
Or any thing I see
He is my Lord and Master
The One of whom I sing
He is my coming King

Merriel Haworth
August 12 - 17

Sweet Rest
He will never leave me nor forsake me
If I always do my best
In His strong and loving arms He'll take me
There I know I shall find sweet rest

Merriel Haworth
October 13th

Baby Doris
(My baby sister, age 2)

Now the rain is pouring down, and it makes me sad
I know that it will sink within the little grave beneath the sod
But oh, when I stop and think she's better off than I
I'm glad to know that she's prepared for that home which is on
high

It was so hard to give her up; she was so dear to me
And the sorrow of our cup, how can so much e'er be
But oh how glad I am to know she so much loved the Lord
And she so much loved to sing and pray, even while going along the
road

She was so sweet and loving kind; and was so very good to mind
She loved to do what Papa said while he was so sick in bed
She was so kind and mighty sweet; it would be awfully hard to
beat
She would say Mama's Kugar, too; without her it is hard to do
Now she is at rest I know; asleep in Jesus here below
Waiting for the home on high; where she will never, never die
Never again will we part there; what happy times await us where
Our blessed Savior will be with us then; and we shall never be
apart again

Merriel English
January 9, 1929

The Blood That Flowed

Jesus wants your hearts my brothers
Oh dear ones no longer wait
If you do, you may regret it
For 'next time' it may be too late

He who came and for you suffered
Wants you for His own today
For He came to bear your burdens
Oh dear friend don't you tell Him, 'nay'

He upon the cross has suffered
He, for you, was crucified
Oh He's lovingly entreating
For your sins He bled and died

Though your sins may be as scarlet
He will make them white as snow
That is why he came and suffered
That is why His blood did flow

Won't you come my brother? Sister?
Won't you come to Him today?
In His arms He'll take and shield you
And will wash your quilt away

When He comes again, my brothers

All God's children then will go
To that land so bright and happy
Where no tears will ever flow

Oh how sad will be that morning
For the ones to whom He'll say
You must depart from Me forever
For you have rejected Me

Oh my friends please don't go with them
With the ones rejecting God
For today there is Salvation
Through His healing, cleansing blood

Merriel Haworth
(Sung to the tune of Broken Engagement)
March 20, 1935

Thank You Lord For Everything
Thank You, Lord, for sun and air
And flowers blooming everywhere
For summer, autumn, winter, spring
And for the songs that we sing
~~*
Thank you Lord, for everything

Merriel Haworth
October 26, 1955

Safe and Secure
Safe and secure in Jesus my Lord
Resting alone on His precious Word
He has redeemed me and loves me I know
By His own blood, which did freely flow.

Merriel Haworth
Sept. 10, 1956

Riding Downstream

Riding downstream,
No effort at all
Just drifting along
Unaware of the fall
I felt so contented
I'm out with the crowd
Doing what they do, oh! I was proud

When suddenly the storm clouds
Seemed hovering near
Somewhere just ahead
It seemed I could hear
The roar of the falls
It seems so near now
I must stop, pull aside
Someone save me now
But who? How?

Now I'm so frightened
Though still in the crowd
There's no one to hear me
Praying aloud
For help from disaster
I'm nearing the fall
Their shrill laughing voices
Drown out my call

Someone help me, oh help me,
Please help me I plead
But my friends are all gone now
I'm alone in my need
I must find escape from the plight that I'm in
For the stream I've been drifting in
Is the dark stream of sin

There must be some one to help me
Somewhere I searched for a friend
I found one in prayer
I found my redeemer, my savior, my guide
He saw my great pride
He heard when I cried

Lord save a poor sinner
I cried to Him
Then he stretched forth his hand
To save me from sin
He's now here beside me
He loves me I know
He'll lead me and guide me
Wherever I go

Merriel's Wedding Picture

Where Are You Headed?
(Sung To: God Is Still On The Throne)

Oh where are you headed, dear brother?
Are you headed for heaven or hell?
Do you have Christ Jesus abiding within you?
Can you say with your soul it is well?

Have you come to the cross of the Savior?
Have you laid all your cares upon Him?
Have you yielded yourself to Him, fully?
Can you say you have victory within?

Merriel Haworth
March 7, 1956

Following Jesus

Jesus take me as I am
Cast all my fears away
Fill me with thy Spirit, Lord
Keep me through each day

In the center of thy will
Help me Lord to do
All the things you bid me Lord
Help me to be true

Lead me; guide me, Lord each day
As through life I go
Hoping, trusting in thy love
More of grace to know

Leading others to Thy throne
By the path You trod
Teaching them to know Thy love
And put their trust in God

And when this life is over, Lord
And in great power you come
May I be ready, Lord to hear
Thy precious words, well done

Come enter into rest, my child
And lay your burden down
For you a crown of life have won
A prize of great renown

Merriel Haworth
02/26/1956

Jesus is the Holy One
The One who answers prayer!
A True Friend

If you are lonely, discouraged and blue
Forsaken by friends and those you thought true
Just remember there's one who's longing to be
The kind of a friend who will not forsake thee

One who is longing to save you from sin
Cleanse your poor soul and give you victory within
Gave His life on the cross that through Him we might live
All glory and honor to Him we should give

One who is coming some day fore His own
To be gathered around Him upon His white throne
To the redeemer of all ages together we'll sing
And crown Him forever our Savior and King

Merriel Haworth
1956

Pentecostal Messengers

The Pentecostal messengers
Are gathered here again
To sing and pray and read God's Word
And let King Jesus reign

We love to work for Jesus
His soldiers here to be
We'll do our part with willing heart
And claim the victory

So come and help us all you can
We each must do our part
To carry on this work for God
And win the sinner's heart

So come and help us all you can
You, too, can help to call
The lost ones to the throne of God
There's rest and peace for all

Merriel Haworth
1956

Special Event

If for some reason
You wish they'd sit still
To save time for some special event
Just say, "Come on folks, lets all testify."
"Take all the time you want."

Most every one will stick real tight to their seat
You could hardly drag anyone to their feet
Everyone will then be content
To leave plenty of time for that special event
Before we dismiss and go home again

Merriel Haworth
February 15, 1959

My Darling I Love You

I miss you so much
I long for your kisses
I long for your touch
It's always so lonely
Since you have been gone
But we'll meet in glory
When God calls me home

Mary Helen Walks The Master's Road
Mary Helen is a lovely girl
Who gave her heart to God
She Is striving day by day to walk
The road the Master trod

Bearing up the heavy cross
Not fainting 'neath the load
While pointing other souls to God
By the straight and narrow road

Merriel Haworth
April 22, 1957
About 1:00 AM

God Bless You
God bless and keep you in His care
And may we in His kingdom
Each have a share

Merriel Haworth
Written for Grandma's New Year's Card
1957-58

Our Pastor

Our Pastor and his lovely wife
And their sweet daughter, too
We've learned to love them very much
For all the things they do

To help us keep in touch with God
Lest from the path we stray
To lead along the path He trod
They work by night and day

A word of courage here and there
A song, a prayer, a tear
A message from the Word of God
To let us know He's near

To let us know He loves us all
To let us know He cares
To let us know He died for all
And all our burden shares

Some day our God will give reward
To soldiers such as they
When He returns to earth again
And takes us home to stay

So let's be faithful, you and I
And help them share the load
Help bring others to The Way
And point them to the road

That leads us to that home above
Prepared for us on high
Where all is joy, and peace, and love
And none shall ever die

Merriel Haworth
April 22, 1957

Shove with Love

We should get behind our pastor
And shove when the road is steep
Not lag behind and weigh him down
With the trifles we try to keep

But cast away the useless things
That complicate our life
And make his load more heavy
Because they stir up strife
Lets learn to love each other
And black the devils eye
By living a pure and holy life
Pleasing to God on high

Don't talk about each other
Or listen when others speak
But keep our hearts in tune with God
And pray for those who are weak

Then if we all work together
And each one pull his share
We can lighten the load of our pastor
And let him know we care
M.H.
March 1, 1959

Sought By The Master
In my youth I was a Christian
And I loved my Savior dear
Loved to read His Holy Bible
Loved to do His precious will

Then one day I wandered from Him
Wandered far from the Master's fold
And I stumbled in the darkness
Lost my way out in the cold

But He loved me and He sought me
'Til He found me in despair
Put His loving arms around me
And shouldered all my care

As He leads me gently over
All the rough and rugged road
And I find the journey easy
For He carries all the load

Merriel Haworth
April 22, 1957

Baby Boy Forest

There is a darling baby
That I'd love to see today
A precious little, baby boy
They named him Forest Jay
His father is my nephew
That makes his mother my dear niece
I know they love him very much
He brings such joy to each

He has two brothers and two sisters
We love them, every one
Some day there may be others
To join them in their fun
As they romp and play together
Be it morning noon or night
Just now perhaps a peaceful scene
But then a little fight

They named him Forest for his uncle
That's why I'm so proud, you see
Who is his aunt who loves him so?
Why don't you know?
That's ME!

Merriel Haworth
April 1957

I Will Praise My Blessed Savior
He has done so much for me
For He pardoned all my sinning
When He died on Calvary

Oh I love Him, yes I love Him
For He came and set me free
Free from all the sin that bound me
When He died on Calvary

I am going to that city
Where the streets are paved with gold
Where the flowers bloom forever
And we'll never more grow old

Won't you come and join that number
Of redeemed ones gathering in?
When the blessed Savior calls us
And we'll all be free from sin

For I know that over yonder
On that day so bright and fair
We will all be glad we entered
For we'll meet our Savior there

Merriel Haworth
5-17-1957

Happy at Last

He'll bear you up safely and carry you through
And after the storm is all past
You'll find He has worked it all out for the best
And you will be happy at last

Happy in Jesus, for His way is best
You've been tried as by fire
And stood firm in the test

So look up, dear child
And have faith in God
All will work out for the best
When we trust in the Lord

Merriel Haworth
July 7, 1957

Safe From The Storm

The storm clouds are gathering
High up in the sky
The coming of Jesus
Is drawing so nigh
You'd better get ready
To meet our dear Lord
'Ere the storm overtakes
And you're lost in the flood

If you don't want to be
Lost in the storm
Then hide you in Jesus
Where naught can cause alarm
Safe and secure in God's wondrous love
Some day to dwell in
Bright mansions up above

Jesus, my Savior, is
Loving and kind
None to compare
Here on earth you can find
He died on the cross
And shed His own blood
Just to save your poor soul
From sin's dark, raging flood

Come to my Savior, Jesus
Oh sinner, today
List' to His pleading
No longer delay
Come kneel at the altar
And give God your heart
If you but trust Him
Then he'll do His part

When you have given
Your heart to my Lord
Repented form your sins
And believed on His Word
Yielded to Him
If you only obey
He'll baptize with His Spirit
Oh, do not delay

Merriel Haworth
May 1957

He is There

1.) Jesus is near though dark seems the way. And everything seems to go wrong. When loved ones forsake us and turn us away. He still fills our heart with a song

Chorus: For His love is dearer than all we have known. He shares every burden we bear. He'll pilot us safely through life's darkest storm. When a friend's needed most, He is there.

2.) If we trust Him, with our hand in His, we can conquer life's darkest storm. For He is our strength, our refuge and friend, just lean on His strong loving arm.

Chorus: For His love is dearer than all we have known. He shares every burden we bear. He'll pilot us safely through life's darkest storm. When a friend's needed most, He is there.

3.) He'll bear you up safely and carry you through. And after the storm is all past you'll find He has worked it all out for your best. And you will be happy at last.

Chorus: For His love is dearer than all we have known. He shares every burden we bear. He'll pilot us safely through life's darkest storm. When a friend's needed most, He is there.

4.) Happy in Jesus, for His way is best. You've been tried by the fire and stood firm the test. So look up, dear child, and have faith in our God, and all will work out for the best when we trust in the Lord.

Chorus: For His love is dearer than all we have known. He shares every burden we bear. He'll pilot us safely through life's darkest storm. When a friend's needed most, He is there.

Merriel Haworth
July 7, 1957

My Strength

He's my strength and my refuge
My shelter from the storm
He'll shield and protect me
And keep me from all harm

He leads me through the pastures
So rich and so green
With the sweetest beauty
That I have ever seen

Then holds my hand so gently
And shoulders the load
When steep is the hill
And rough is the road

Merriel Haworth
July 16, 1957

Are You Heavy Hearted?

Are you heavy hearted?
Are you burdened down with care?
Do you think your load of trouble
Is far more than you can bear?
Do you feel you are forsaken?
All alone on this old earth?
Void of love and understanding,
Void of laughter, song and mirth?
Do you think there is no answer?
None to help you, none to care?
Just bring your cares to Jesus
He's a friend that's always there
He will love and understand you
He will save your soul from sin
He will heal your broken spirit
Give you joy and peace within

Merriel Haworth
July 16, 1957

If I

I may stumble, I may fall
It doesn't matter after all
If I rise and do my best
To follow Him and pass each test
He will take my hand and lead me
He will care for me and feed me
If I put my faith and trust in Him alone

When I feel the need of comfort
From the daily pressures and hurt
That comes from my turmoil and my strife
He's my Savior; He's my guide
From the storms I safely hide
In the arms of Jesus Christ, my truest friend
If I let Him fill my heart and soul and life

If I do my best Him to serve
From His path try not to swerve
Doing all to meet His calling
From the heights I'll not be falling
He will take my hand and guide me
In His arms He'll safely hide me
When I leave this world and follow Him alone

Merriel Haworth
November 5, 1957

How Sweet

How sweet the name of Jesus is
I love Him more each hour
How sweet to know that I am His
He keeps me by His power

How sweet to put my trust in God
To know He answers prayer
How sweet to walk the path He trod
And know I'm in His care

How sweet to know that some glad day
He'll come and take me home
Then in this sinful world below
I never more shall roam

I'll be home with Christ, my Lord
In mansions bright and fair
I'll walk the streets of gold
And all His glory share

How sweet if I should meet you there
My Jesus loves you, too
So lean upon His tender care
And He will welcome you

Such joy there is in serving God
You'll be so glad you came
To rest upon His tender care
And trust in His dear name

Merriel Haworth
November 13, 1957

The Missionary's Message

When the missionary returned to Pomona
From the lands across the sea
And I heard the verses of Scripture
As he talked to you and to me

My heart was stirred with the message
Of our Savior, so precious and dear
Who left His home in glory
And came to dwell with us here

To fulfill the plans of His Father
To spread the gospel about
So the people know of Salvation
And their hearts be filled with a shout

He walked and He talked with the people
He taught them of God and His love
And He said if we prove ever faithful
We shall dwell in bright mansions above

He opened blind eyes as He journeyed
He healed the sick and the lame
And we can be healed, dear brother
If we ask and believe in His name

He died on the cross to save us
Fulfilling God's great plans
In shame He suffered and died there
With nail through His feet and His hands

He paid the debt for our sinning
As He hung on 'the old rugged cross'
That whosoever believeth in Him
Shall not go down with the lost

Merriel Haworth
November 19, 1957
At Church during a message by Brother Hughes – a missionary.
Nothing Compares

- 33 -

Won't You Join Me?

As I hold Jesus' hand in my own
And talk with my Savior as He sits on his throne
His love will surround me; no joy can compare
With the joy that awaits me when I get up there

If you would avoid being lost in the storm
Then come into the shelter of His loving arms
He'll take you and shield you in His wondrous love
And prepare you to dwell in bright mansions above

Come kneel at the altar and be cleansed from your sin
Get His forgiveness and have sweet peace within
He'll save you and keep you under His wing
All glory and honor give to Jesus our King

Then you must live daily close to the Lord
Kneel often in prayer and study His word
Do what He bids you and tell others, too
And remember that Jesus will never forsake you

Oh the great joy that awaits us in heaven up yonder
And the peace that He gives us is beyond all wonder
Oh the wondrous love that He gives cannot be compared
And it is beyond our imagination that Jesus should care

Merriel Haworth
December 20, 1957

That Promised Land

When the Messiah shall come to receive us and take us
To dwell in bright mansions, fair
From trials and tests He then shall relieve us
And all of His glory then we shall share

We'll leave this old world so far behind us
And rise to meet Jesus high up in the air
We'll go with our Savior to that prepared city
And then we'll forever abide with Him there

We'll walk and we'll talk with bright angels in glory
And walk upon streets that are paved with pure gold
We'll shout and we'll sing that grand old, sweet story
How Jesus redeemed us and we'll never grow old

We'll meet His disciples who journeyed back yonder
We'll meet our dear loved ones, who've gone on before
All will be love and peace and such gladness
As we meet Jesus when this life is o're

Oh won't it be wondrous to be with our Savior
To talk with the angels to join heaven's band
To meet our dear loved ones who've gone on before us
To walk golden streets in that Promised Land

Merriel Haworth
Dec. 20, 1957

A Friend That's Always There

Are you heavy hearted
Burdened down with Care
Do you think your load of trouble
Is much more than you can bear
Do you feel forsaken
All alone on this old earth
Void of love and understanding
Void of laughter, sang and mirth

Do you think there is no answer
None to help you; none to care
Just bring your cares to Jesus
He's a Friend that's always there
He will love and understand you
He will save your soul from sin
He will heal your broken spirit
Give you peace and joy within

Merriel Haworth
1957

These Lovely Gifts
For these lovely gifts
I thank you, everyone
It's been a lovely party
And I've hade lots of fun

And when I use each of these gifts
I'll think of he who gave it
And when it's worn completely out
I expect that I'll still save it

Merriel Haworth
March 18, 1958

Dear Jim, And Lill...
Dear Jim and Lill and babies three
As sweet a family as ever I did see
We feel so bad you are away
When you come again we will be more gay
We hope you'll be with us soon again
Your presence will then relieve the pain
Our parting caused when you went away
I hope when you come it will be to stay
For we love you so and we want you near
To fill our hearts and home with cheer
But, although we love you and want you too
We want most of all what is best for you.

Merriel Haworth
April 9, 1958

Party Invitation
To Honor The Birth Of:
Michael Wayne McDaniel

We're inviting you; oh joy, oh joy
To buy a gift for a tiny boy
Then meet at the home of my mother, sweet
At 237 East Maple Street
In Ontario, Cali-for-ni-a
We hope that the party will be quite gay
To give these gifts to Michael Wayne McDaniel
Who came on August ___, 1958
To bless the home of Earl and Barbara McDaniel
The party to be given on October 4th
By none other than the Haworth's

Merriel Haworth
Aug or Oct 1958

Answering God's Call

She is standing by the window
As the night winds kissed her cheek
And she waited all in silence
Waited long, e'er she could speak

Then at long last she whispered softly
Yes, my Lord, I hear your call
I have lived a life so sinful
Now, dear Lord, I'll leave it all

I will leave my home and loved ones
I will go and work for Thee
In foreign lands across the waters
Here I am, dear Lord, send me

For I know that's where You've called me
I am ready now to go
And help lead others to Thy kingdom
Why, oh why was I so slow

Many there must now have perished
While I waited, loath to go
I must hurry now to warn them
For You love them all I know

The harvest now is ripe and waiting
Wasting while I here delay
Many precious souls have perished
Please forgive me now, I pray

Merriel Haworth
Aug. 14, 1958

Hold steady in the boat
Don't lose your grip
We must keep afloat
For this great trip

This trip will lead us home
To mansions fair above
We sail the sea of life
Secure in the Master's love

Don't fear or falter row the boat
The course keep straight and true
Our Master's sailed this way before
To make a way for you

The storms may rage the winds may blow
The waves pile high and wide
Just row, pull steady firm and true
Our blessed Lord is nigh

He'll see you safely through the storm
Don't lose your faith in Him
Just hold His hand and brave the storm
And leave behind all sin

Hold steady friend, hold steady
We must not rock the boat
Look up, have faith, obey His will
We must, MUST keep afloat

Merriel Haworth
Aug. 26, 1958

How most of us remember our Auntie.

Like Jesus

I love my dear Jesus, I love Him
I want to be like Him, I do
I want to go be with my Savior
I want to lead others there, too

So won't you come join in the journey
Toward Heaven's bright mansions, above
And help me to spread this glad story
And share in the depths of His love

Merriel Haworth
Aug. 1958

Missionary Pledge

Because my waistline is inclined to vary
I send this much to the Missionary
Now I'm not this big, you can plainly see
But still there's way too much of me

With a prayer to speed across the wave
Along with the offering others gave
May it help bring cheer to the loyal heart
Of the Missionary who has a part

Of saving the souls of those that be
In foreign lands across the sea
May God bless each and every one
'Till we meet in heaven with the victory won

Merriel Haworth
Sept. 1958

The Hollow Of His Hand

Jesus never fails
When the storms are raging high
To lift us up above the clouds
Until the storms go by

If we will keep our eyes on Him
And never trust in man
He'll keep us safe, secure and warm
In the hollow of His hand

Merriel Haworth
Oct 26, 1958

God's Hand

I was ready to enter the gates of hell
When God reached out a loving hand
Saying; 'that's not for you, oh child of mine'
'I'll lead you to a far better land'
'Just hold fast my hand and follow my steps'
'Have faith and trust in my might'
'I'll lead you to joys that have never been told'
'I'll lead you through darkness to a bright, shining light'

I turned and I saw He was speaking to me
'Twas to me He was saying; 'come home'
'I love you dear child; I want you for my own'
'No longer this downward pathway to roam'
So I turned my steps upward to follow His steps
And now with my hand in His own
He leads me through valleys and high mountaintops
On this journey toward heaven and home

I'll follow wherever He leads me, I know
Though darkness assails me and death hovers near
All things work together for good to His own
He'll never send more than I'm able to bear
He molds me and shapes me through trials and tests
And then when the molding is done
I'll shine as pure gold; refined by His hand
Worthy to wear the crown I have won

Merriel Haworth
October 5, 1958

Do We Have To Be Of This World?

'Tis a wicked world we live in
But do we have to be wicked, too?
Do we have to do the things that we see others do?

Do we have to say the naughty words
That we hear others say?
Do we have to go the places
Where we see their feet stray?

Do we have to seek our pleasures
Where the world is seeking theirs?
Just travel on the crowded way
Thinking that there's no one who cares?

NO, there's a loving Savior
Who sees everything we do
He hears every word we utter
He sees every where we go

He tells us that He loves us
He has made for us a way
Where we'll find far greater pleasures
Than the world finds here today

We can tell them that He loves them, too
And take them by the hand
And strive to take them there with us
To that blessed, Promised Land

We can find sweet pleasures
In serving Christ, our Lord
We can fine great treasures
As we share His word

We can enter Holy places
As we go in prayer
We can have our sins forgiven
And find sweet communion there

We can go and serve Him daily
As we go upon our way
And tell others of the blessings
That we find in Him today

Which Road Will You take

There's a highway to heaven
'Twas built by God's hand
With sign posts to lead us
To that Promised Land

A land of great beauty
Which none can compare
With God's hand to lead us
As we journey there

The highway's a straight way
And narrow is the road
But someone to help us
With each heavy load

He walks close beside us
Each step of the way
He leads us through darkness
To a much brighter day

He will never forsake us
But lead us straight on
With love and forgiveness
'Till victory is won

There's a broad way leads downward
To pain and despair
And many, so many
Are traveling there

Great dangers await them
They seem not to heed
The signposts that warn them
They won't stop and read

They travel so gaily
This broad, downward road
That leads to destruction
And the wrath of our God

The devil will tell them
That they don't need to pray

Or study God's Holy Bible
Just go the broad way

They'll find the old devil
Is just a big liar
He'll lead them to ruin
And into the fire

The highway to heaven
The broad way to hell
Oh friend, dear friend
Consider it well

Which road are you traveling?
Which way will you go?
The way that leads upward
Or the one down below?

'Tis the most serious choice
We each one must make
Ponder it well my friend
Don't make a mistake

Don't take the broad way
That's been traveled so well
That leads to destruction
And lands you in hell

But take a straight narrow way
To heaven up above
To be with our Savior
In joy, peace, and love

Merriel Haworth
Oct. 1958

Though He Slay Me

Though He slay me, yet I will trust Him
As was spoken by Job long ago
What ever He sends I knows for the best
When He calls for me, I'm ready to go

But if He should take the ones I love best
And leave me here 'till the last
He'll never send more than I'm able to bear
He'll see me through every test

Though He slays me, yet I will trust Him
'Twas spoken by Job long ago
And I feel the same of my Redeemer and King
For He loves me, I surely do know

If He should take the dearest on earth
Whatever He chooses is best
He'll never send more than I'm able to bear
He'll see me through every hard test

Whenever He calls me I'm ready to go!

Merriel Haworth
Oct. 1958

My Honey
(For Markie)

My honey, my honey
So precious and sweet
My honey, my honey
I think you're so neat
My honey, my honey
There's none can compete
With my honey, my honey
So precious and sweet

Merriel Haworth
Nov. 19, 1958

Scents Or Cents?
Since I cannot smell
I believe you can tell
My dear, I mean no offense

But I got it on sale
And here's the good tale
So I saved not dollars, but cents

Merriel Haworth

Evangelists
We love the Evangelist Ministers
We love the message they bring
From the Word of our Heavenly Father
We love the songs that they sing
We listen so very intently
To each and every last word
As we enjoy the blessings flowing
Our hearts are being stirred
We fall on our knees at the altar
And pour out our hearts to God

Merriel Haworth
January 1959

Jesus is . . .
Jesus is the way maker
He made a way for you
Jesus is the sin taker
He bore it all for you

Jesus is the sick healer
He wants to heal you, too
Jesus is the soul saver
He'll cleanse you through and through

Jesus is the one who died
Upon the cruel tree
He freely gave His life's blood
To ransom you and me

Jesus is the Son God gave
To bring Salvation free
And when He comes in glory
His blessed face we'll see

Merriel Haworth
January 28, 1959

Testimony, Anyone?
When the testimonies lag and the services drag
Just say, 'folks we haven't much time'
We must cut this part of the service short
And save our testimonies for another time

Then up pops this one and up pops that one
Someone will preach and then
Most everyone here has testified
If the preacher has time, he can say a word
Before we dismiss and go home again

Merriel Haworth
February 15, 1959

Am I Perfect?

Am I perfect?
God forbid I should claim to be
When there's so much that shows in my life
That is only me

God grant
That I might lay aside
The part that is only me
And let my heart be filled complete
With things that are of Thee

Help me
To grow, dear Lord, in Thee
That I might fruitful be
That I might do Thy will always
And perfect myself in Thee

Mar 8, 1959

Testimony

You can stand up in church and testify
And make folks think you live "just so"
But what you are outside the church
Folks outside the church will know

So it behooves us, every one
To search our hearts and see
If we're the same inside the church
As where the world can see

Can we be glad to know
Our life's an open book?
Is each page clean and pure
So we don't care who takes a look?

If we can't feel that way, my friend
Then God wants us to go
Upon our knees and repent of sin
And let His blessings flow

To cleanse our hearts and make folks see
Christ in everything we do
So they will want to leave all sin
And live for Jesus, too!

Merriel Haworth
March 13, 1959

Have You . . .

Have you grieved the Holy Spirit?
Have you wounded the heart of our Lord?
Have you forgotten to pray and seek Him?
Forgotten to read His Word?

Have you drifted along with the current,
Away from our Savior's love?
Neglected to meet with His people?
Neglected that home above?

There's forgiveness, if you ask Him
With repentant and contrite heart
If you will meet the conditions
Then God will do His part

He never forsaketh His children
He loves you and His love is true
He offers forgiveness for asking
Repentance MUST come from you!

Merriel Haworth
June 9, 1959

Take Him

We can take Him on the highway
We can take Him on the byway
We can take Him on the freeway
And then

He'll be with you where you go
And this one thing I know
We can take Him when we go
Back home again

Merriel Haworth
June 28, 1959

He Did This For Me

Glory to Jesus, our Savior and King
Gladly His praises forever I'll sing

Redeemed by the blood that He shed on that tree
Wonderful mercy, He did this for me!

Merriel Haworth
September 1, 1959

Tears

Tears that touch the heart of God
Oh that such tears would flow
More freely from the eyes of those
Who claims our Christ to know

Beseeching God for those who stray
Away from the Master's fold
To bring them in and secure them there
In bonds of Love to hold

Don't be ashamed of tears, my friend
Just let the teardrops fall
They'll touch the heart of God, I know
Christ died to save us all

Merriel Haworth
June 28, 1959

Are You Heavy Hearted?

Are you heavy hearted
Are you burdened down with care
Do you think your load of trouble
Is far more that you can bear

Do you feel you are forsaken
All alone on this old earth
Void of love and understanding
Void of laughter, song and mirth

Just bring your cares to Jesus
He's a friend that's always there
He will love and understand you
He will save your soul from sin
He will heal your broken spirit
Give you joy and peace within

Merriel Haworth
July 16, 1959
In church Sunday night

Some Glad Day

How sweet to know that some glad day
My Lord shall carry me away

And take me where I then shall be
In heaven for all eternity

I'll meet my loved ones over there
Who are waiting for me, safe in His care

Merriel Haworth
June 27, 1959

Jesus Is Coming

Jesus is coming
Some day for His own
He'll gather them 'round Him
As He sits on His throne

We'll sing glad hosanna's
To Jesus our King
Sweetly the voices
In heaven shall ring

Merriel Haworth
September 1, 1959

Jesus Is Longing
Oh lift up your head
And rejoice all ye people
For Jesus is longing
To save you from sin
Oh lift up your head
And rejoice al ye people
He's longing and waiting
To cleanse you within

Oh do not reject Him
Just kneel and accept Him
He's longing and waiting
To save you from sin

Oh do not reject Him
Come kneel and accept Him
For Jesus is waiting
To save you from sin

Merriel Haworth
September 10, 1956

Let Christ

Jesus is calling the weary to rest
Repent of your sins and lean on His breast
He offers forgiveness, 'tis yours to obey
To kneel at the altar, let God have His way

There's peace for the mind
There's rest for the soul
There's healing for the body
Let Christ make you whole

Oh yield yourself to Him
Find strength for each test
For Jesus is calling the weary to rest

There's peace for the mind
There's rest for the soul
There's healing for the body
Let Christ have control

Merriel Haworth

Take Time To Pray

I stood at the sink in the kitchen
The dishes stacked high in the pan
My work must be finished e'er nighttime
I must hurry as fast as I can

The beds must be made, I must hurry
The floors must be scrubbed, yet, today
So much to be done, the clothes must be hung
I cannot take time now to pray

So I hurried and tired to work faster
But everything seemed to go wrong
I'd neglected to talk with the Master
And then I thought of this song

Take time to pray in the morning
And Christ will be with you all day
Work's to be done
Or you're just seeking fun
Always take time first to pray

So I left my work there, yet unfinished
And knelt by the bedside to pray
Oh my soul got so happy
I stayed there 'most half the day

Merriel Haworth
Sept 30, 1959

When God Comes In, Giants Get Out
There are giants roaming the land today
These giants hinder in every way
God's spirit from reaching the heart of man
They will keep us from God if they can

But God is stronger than giants, you see
His love reaches out for you and for me
These giants hinder the Christian life
Hatred, envy, malice and strife

We must slay these giants, if you please
With the weapon of prayer, while down on our knees
With the Sword of god's Word we can put them to route
When God comes in, these giants will go out!

Merriel Haworth
Oct. 25, 1959

Jesus Use Me

Jesus use my hands today
Help them, dear Lord, to do
Some kind and loving deed, dear Lord
To point someone to You

Jesus use my lips today
Help them, dear Lord, to say
Some kind and loving word, dear Lord
To help them on their way

Jesus use my feet today
Help them, dear Lord, to go
Upon Your mission here, dear Lord
That others, too, may know

Jesus use me as I am
My hands, my lips, my feet
That I may show Thy Word, Thy love
To those I chance to meet

Merriel Haworth
Nov. 10, 1959

Drifting

I've been drifting with the current
Just drifting with the tide
With my eyes closed to the dangers
Of taking such a ride

Not praying much to God above
Reading not His Holy Word
Just drifting, slowly drifting
'Till today His voice I heard

Warning me that I must waken
Of my plight, take heed
That I must pray with earnest heart
And His Holy Word must read

If I would set my heart at rest
And safely reach the shore
If I would pass each coming test
I must trust my Savior more

Merriel Haworth
1959

What I want to say
I love You, Daddy
You're the BEST Dad I know
There couldn't be a nicer one
Where ever I go

Do these words sound familiar, Dad?
Words I said so long ago
But I love you just as much, Dad
As I did then, you know

Though the wheel chair has held you
So long now, dear Dad
You're still the BEST Daddy
A girl (boy/guy) ever had

There may be a wrinkle
A gray hair or so
But each year you grow dearer
And dearer, you know

God gave me the best Dad
So again just let me say
I love you so, Daddy
On this Father's Day – and every Day!

Merriel Haworth
Father's Day 1962

Keep The Wheel A Turning
There's a stream of water flowing
From the throne to us, today
It keeps the wheel a turning
As long as we will always pray

And trust our heavenly Father
With our hand placed in His own
As long as the wheel's a turning
Our sins will all be gone

But if we fail to kneel and pray
We lose our faith in Him
The wheel will stop a turning
And sin will soon creep in

Let's keep the wheel a turning
And keep our faith in God
To give us power to stay upon
The path our Master's trod

And power to help someone to find
That stream of water, too
That stream that shall not e'er run dry
That flows for me and you

Let's give that wheel an extra turn
By extra prayers today
We need the power God has for us
Let's let Him have His way!

Merriel Haworth
Feb. 2, 1960

From Brother Burrages' Sermon
Life's Road
If your feet begin to stagger
And you sink beneath the load
Of sin's burden heaped upon you
As you travel on life's road

Filled with thorns, so rough and rugged
Dark and stormy; filled with fear
Sinking deeper, ever deeper
Sick with worry, heartache, tears

Don't despair, my weary brother
Lift your head and look to Him
Who Himself sank even deeper
Yet did not give way to sin

Though He bore sin's heavy burden
Bore it all for you and me
That we might receive our pardon
Ever died on Calvary

Knowing this, that Jesus suffered
As He traveled on this road
Bore the heavy cross to Calvary
That He staggered 'neath the load

As His steps drew ever nearer
Going there His life to give
Crowned with thorns, His head bowed in prayer
All of this that we might live

Will you then, my weary brother
Travel on this downward road
Shunning all the love He offered
When He wants to share your load

Oh forsake sin's way forever
Turn your face toward heaven above
Bask you in the heavenly sunlight
Of our Lord's eternal love

Merriel Haworth
September – October 1960

'Neath The Load

If your feet begin to stagger
And you sink beneath the load
Burden heaped upon you
As you travel on life's road
Filled with thorns, so rough and rugged
Dark and stormy, filled with fears
Sinking deeper, even deeper
Sick with worry, heartache, tears

Don't despair, my weary brother
Lift your head and look to Him
Who Himself sank even deeper
Yet did not give way to sin
Tho' He bore sin's heavy burden
Bore it all for you and me
That we might receive our pardon
Even died on Calvary

Knowing this, that Jesus suffered
As He traveled on this road
Bore the heavy cross to Calvary
That He staggered 'neath the load
As His steps drew even nearer
Going there, His life to give
Innocent blood was shed there, brother
All of this that we might live

Will you then, my weary brother
Travel on this downward road?
Shunning all the love He offered
When He wants to share your load?
Oh, forsake sin's ways forever
Turn your face toward heaven above
Bask you in the heavenly sunlight
Of the Lord's eternal love

Let Him take your hand and gently
Lead you on from day to day
Sharing all your heavy burdens
As you travel on life's way

He'll forgive you if you ask Him
He will save your soul from sin
Open now your heart to Jesus
Open wide and let Him in!

Merriel Haworth
Sept & Oct 1961

Heavenly Blessings
In Pomona at sixth and Linden
A little church house stands
Inside you can hear singing
That sounds like angel bands

Such blessings flow from heaven
Rich gifts from God, in His love
Just a little taste of what's waiting
In that beautiful home above

Merriel Haworth
March 11, 1962

Daddy

Hi Daddy, how are you?
Did you know this is your day?
Bend down, Daddy, let me whisper
My Own Dear Daddy

As I sit and ponder this evening
Of the special day at hand
I'm thinking of the nicest Father
The sweetest Dad in all the land

A Dad who's been kind and patient
Though his body's been wracked with pain
And been handicapped in a wheelchair
When he's longing to be free again

I'm thinking of my own dear Daddy
As this Father's Day draws near
And the love in my heart gets stronger
As I think of you, Daddy Dear

You're smiling presence to cheer us
A kind word or two when we're sad
And yes, your firm hand of correction
To set us right when we're bad

I loved you so in my childhood
And when it seemed you didn't care
But I love you more even now, Dad
Though you've a few silver threads in your hair

From the scenes of my childhood 'till now, Dad
How the years swiftly come and go
Still my darling Dad in his wheelchair
Beat all other Dads I know

Merriel Haworth
Father's Day, June 1962

Oh taste and see that the Lord is good;
Blessed is the man that trusteth in Him
Psalms 34:8

New Wine

It's the new wine I'm drinking of
It's the new wine from heaven above
It's the new wine; it's the new wine that I'm drinking of

A fountain was opened at Pentecost
Now it's flowing for all the lost
It's the new wine; it's the new wine that I'm drinking of

A favorite chorus of:
Merriel Haworth
March 11, 1962

I Repent

I've been sitting home each evening
Feeling sorry for myself
Instead of reading God's Holy Word
It lies there on the shelf

It seemed I was forsaken
I even murmured and complained
But, now I know the ground I've lost
The devil must have gained

I haven't talked much with my Lord
I'm so ashamed now, you see
For even though I've neglected Him
He never has neglected me

As I sat writing this in church tonight
Listening to others testify
I went down on my knees to pray
To humble myself and cry

Father forgive my selfish ways
My leaving you up on the shelf
I wasn't giving you my praise
I kept it all inside myself

I repent!

Merriel Haworth
September 9, 1962

The Rose

The devil sees this rose, so fair
Shining for God above
But he can't stand this beauty
So he starts in to shove

He pits his strength at the beautiful rose
And shoves with all his might
'Till the rose forgets that God is his strength
And begins to shake with fright

The trials come like falling rain
To shake the rose so fair
He starts to murmur and complain
The strength I had went where?

The cries of this rose
Went on for days the same
And so the broken heart
Thought the answer never came

It seems that a gopher has come
To attack that heart so dear
But I know that God in His mercy
Is always very near

To fill the heart of this rose
With new life from above
And strengthen again the rose
With his never failing love

But Jesus is the answer
He loves the beautiful rose
And though the flower lost its life
Its fragrance ever sweeter grows

For Jesus left His glory
In heaven up above
To come and bring us life anew
For He is Life and Love

Merriel Haworth
Nov. 11, 1964

Scatter Sunshine

If you wish to scatter sunshine
All along your journey here
If you wish to light a face with smiles
Or wipe away a tear
If you wish to lift a burden
And lighten someone's load
Just keep a smile upon your face
And sing along the road

Scatter sunshine daily
With your smiles and with your song
Knowing Jesus loves you
And you know you can't go wrong
As long as Jesus holds your hand
And leads you all the way
So scatter sunshine, sing and smile
And bring more cheer to others Everyday

If you practice this each day
Although your way seems rough
With Jesus walking by your side
You'll find He is enough
To keep that smile upon your face
That song within your heart
So let Him always hold your hand
And never from Him part

Merriel Haworth
Feb. 16, 1964

That Light

I see a Light shining down from heaven
It's the Light of His word that God has given

Saying follow that Light to the end of the day
If you follow that Light it will show you the way

The way to that home in heaven above
That home which abounds in peace and love

The love of our Father, our Savior, our God
So, let's follow that road that our Savior has trod

Merriel Haworth
Feb. 7, 1965

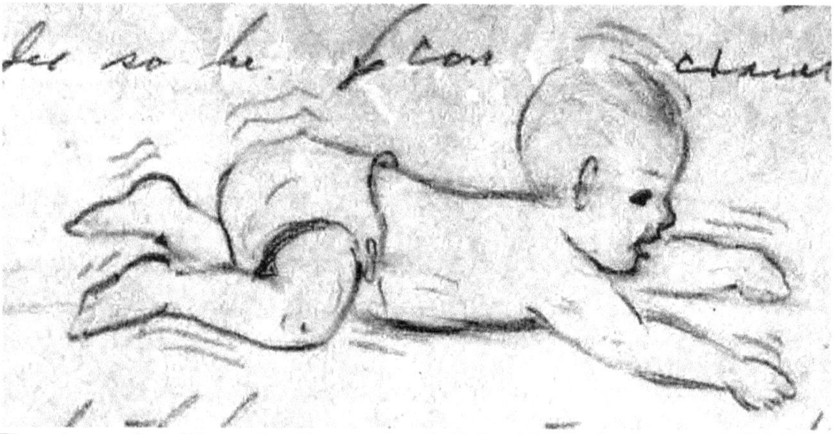

The handwritten text around this drawing says "When he is on his tummy, he scrunches up like this, to get his knees up under so he can crawl.
After his bath he goes out every day and watches the chickens. He looks solemn with big eyes. Then jumps and trips and goes home."
I don't know who this is supposed to be.

At Church
Feel The Spirit Moving

Oh, I feel the Spirit moving in my soul
Stretch out your hand, my friend, and be made whole

He has come to save the lost
He alone has paid the cost

Oh, I feel the Spirit moving in my soul

Merriel Haworth
Feb. 18, 1965

Just Lean on Him

Just lean on His eternal arm
He'll give you strength to bear
The sorrow in you heart, today
We know that He doth care

He sees each tear drop in your eye
The sadness in your heart
He knows how hard it is to bear
When loved ones from us part

He is our strength and refuge, dear
Just trust His love divine
He'll wipe those tear drops from your eyes
Your heart won't have to pine

So put your trust in Him, dear child
And trust His love divine
And lean upon His breast, secure
Then all else will be fine

Merriel Haworth
03-1965

Journey Complete

Lord, help me to follow
The path that You have trod
Yielding my will unto
The very will of God

Help me to humble
Myself at Thy feet
'Till I rest in Thy kingdom
My journey now complete

Merriel Haworth
Oct. 12, 1965

Oh Jesus, Sweet Jesus

Oh Jesus, sweet Jesus
The lover of my soul
Oh Jesus, sweet Jesus
Help me to reach that goal
To enter that city
Made by Thy hand, so fair
Oh Jesus, sweet Jesus
I hope to meet Thee there

Merriel Haworth
Jan. 17, 1966

Thank You Jesus

Thank you Jesus, thank you Jesus
Thank you Jesus, thank you Lord
Thank you for your might power
Thank you for Thy Holy Word

Keep Your hand upon me, Jesus
Be my strength and be my guide
Fill me with Thy Holy Spirit
Ever be close by my side

Thank you Jesus, thank you Jesus
Thank you Jesus, thank you Lord
Thank you for your mighty power
Thank you for Thy Holy Word

Dwell within my heart, Dear Jesus
Make me what I ought to be
Keep me in the "straight and narrow"
'Till Thy shining face I see

Thank you Jesus, thank you Jesus
Thank you Jesus, thank you Lord
Thank you for your might power
Thank you for Thy Holy Word

Merriel Haworth
Feb. 2, 1966
(Chorus – some time ago)

Black Or White

Some skin is black
While some is white
But who'd know the difference
In the dark of night

God looks at the heart
To know if we're clean
The color of the skin
Need not be seen

He knows if we're living
As we should
He knows our deeds
Whether evil or good

If we live for Christ
Then have no fear
Whether black or white
Our God is near

Merriel Haworth
May 23, 1966

Heaven's Light

Oh, I love to praise the Lord
Sing and shout and read God's Word
There's a light down in the valley, now I see

Oh, I love to walk the road
That my Lord and Savior trod
There's a light down in the valley now for me

I was burdened down with sin
'Till my Savior took me in
And from sin and shame He set my spirit free

He loosed the bond of sin that day
When He showed me the way
And at home in heaven, some day I'm sure I'll be

He's my Savior, He's my guide
And I'm oh so satisfied
Since the light down in the valley now I see

He leads me on, He holds my hand
As I journey to that Land
Where the light of heaven shines so bright for me

Merriel Haworth
April 16, 1967

His Love

The Son of God came from above
To bring to us Eternal Love

He died upon the cruel tree
To show His love to you and me

He loved us so He could not see
Us go into eternity

With out a chance to save our soul
So He died and rose to make us whole

Merriel Haworth
Dec. 1966

My Mother

My mother, God bless her
I love her so dear
She means more to me
Year after year

She rocked me to sleep
In her arms, long ago
She loves me even now
As she did then, I know

Merriel Haworth
May 6, 1967

Again He Lives

I know not what may come tomorrow
But I know that for today
I must follow in the footsteps
Where my Savior led the way
I must follow close beside Him
I must cling unto His hand
Till I reach that far horizon
Over in the Promised Land

I must tell it unto others
How the Savior led the way
How He gave His life to save them
If they only choose this way
Leave this sinful world behind them
Walk upon this narrow road
Cast on Him their every burden
He will lighten every load

Yes He gave His life to save us
But again He lives today
He came forth that day victorious
When the stone was rolled away
He paid the price for our salvation
By His stripes we have been healed
And we'll be with him forever
When His power is revealed

Merriel P Haworth
August 24, 1967

He Cried

He cried, Father forgive them
For they do not know what they do
When they pierced His side
And with thorns they crowned His brow

Merriel Haworth
Oct. 1967

God Said

God said:
Who so ever will let him come to Me
Let him drink of the water of life
It's free!

Merriel Haworth
Dec. 31, 1967

MOTHER

M is for Minding, mending, molding

O is for other things that she's done

T is for Tender, Tucking, Teaching, Tending

H is for her Happy Loving Smile

E is for Every Effort Made

R is for her Real, Loving Heart

Merriel Haworth
May 12, 1968

The Mountaintop

From down in the valley
To the mountaintop
I've started climbing
And I won't stop

'Till I get to the summit
To the highest peak
And find the Glories
Of God that I seek

The glories God promised
To those who care
Enough to labor
That they might share

With Christ of Nazareth
Who came from on high
To redeem us from our sin
There we'll never more die

So I'll steadily climb
And labor with love
To gain a place with
My Savior up above

I've started to climb
And I won't stop
Until I've reached
The mountaintop

Merriel Haworth
March 30, 1969

Written while Brother Ronnie Wilhite was preaching.

Jesus Walks Beside Me
I'll never walk alone
For Jesus walks beside me
How could I ever lose my way?
When He is there to guide me?

He knows each step
He's gone before
He knows the way
He'll guide me safely o're

(Written at O'Connor's)

Merriel Haworth
April 28, 1969

Patrick
Patrick, he's a sweet little guy
Patrick, oh me – oh my
He clutches your heartstrings
With that sweet little smile
To be with my Patrick
I'd walk a mile

(He's only two months old)

Merriel Haworth
May 28, 1969

Who Will You Follow?
The Devil is a sly old fox
But my Lord's much smarter than he
The Devil wants to put me in a box
But my Savior set me free

The Devil says; 'go here, go there'
But my Lord says; 'follow me'
So I'll follow Jesus with out a care
Since now the Light I see!

Searching for That City
I've been searching for that City
Where the streets are paved with gold
Where we'll never more grow weary
And we'll never more grow old

Where we'll meet and greet our loved ones
Who have gone that way, before
Where we'll meet our blessed Savior
And be with Him, forever more

Merriel Haworth
Aug 22, 1969

A Girl Named Suzie

I met a pretty girl
Her name I did not know
But one thing you can't accuse me
And that's of being slow
I met her in the evening
Next day we two were wed
As we approached the altar
This is what she said

My name is Suzie
Pray tell me what's your own
Well, my name is Johnnie
But that I would not own
I said my name is Patrick
Come let me take you home
When she awoke next morning
She found that I had gone

Merriel Haworth
January 22, 1970

A Friend You Can Turn To

There is a friend, one you can turn to
To save you from the dark, storm tossed sea
One who will love you above all others
For He gave His life to save you and me

When you are rejected by one you hold dear
And you feel down trodden, lonely and blue
Remember this friend will always be near
For He dearly loves you, and His love is true

Please come to this friend; let Him hold you fast
Let Him comfort and cheer you in His loving arms
Let Jesus pilot you through life's deepest sorrow
For only in Him can you find peace at last

Merriel Haworth
January 23, 1970

This Little Bookmark

I made this little bookmark
And I expect you're liable
To use it on the pages
Of your treasured Holy Bible

I made it cause I love you
And the greatest love you see
I found in the Holy Bible
Is God's love for you and me

I pray as you use this bookmark
And read the book do dear
Your heart will be drawn closer
To the Precious Jewel rare

The Christ who died to save us
Because He loved us so
He took our place on Calvary
So we won't have to go

Merriel Haworth
April 4, 1970

When His Power Is Revealed

I know not what may come tomorrow
But I know that for today
We must follow in the footsteps
Where our Savior led the way
We must follow close beside Him
We must cling unto His hand
'Till we reach that far horizon
Over in the Promised Land

We must tell it unto others
How the Savior led the way
How He gave His life to save them
If they only choose to pray
Leave the sinful world behind them
Walk upon this narrow road
Cast on Him their every burden
He will lighten every load

Yes He gave His life to save us
But He lives again, today
He came forth that day victorious
When the stone was rolled away
He paid the price for our Salvation
By His stripes we have been healed
And we'll be with Him forever
When His power is revealed

Merriel Haworth
Aug. 24, 1967

The last six lines were written
March 15, 1970

The Hands Of Jesus

The hands of Jesus are extended
With the scars so plain to see
Where the nails so painfully pierced Him
As they nailed Him to the tree

How they mocked Him and they scoffed Him
As with a spear they pierced His side
We should love our blessed Savior
And in Him we should abide

Behold, the hands of Jesus
Outstretched and pleading just for thee
He wants you to know He loves you
For you He died upon the tree

Earnestly He beckons you onward
Oh won't you listen to His plea
"Come place your hands into My own;
For I have done all this for thee!"

Would you take the hands of Jesus?
Or mock Him like those who've gone before
He came to earth to give us victory
So we can live with Him forevermore

Merriel Haworth
March 1970

The First Space Man

The very first man in outer space
Was the One who set the world in place.

Merriel Haworth
July 9, 1972

Precious Treasure

Of all my earthly treasures
The most priceless thing I own
Is this precious little Bible
That I call my very own

Merriel Haworth
Sept. 13, 1970

Two Lonely People

Two lonely people, just sitting alone
Longing to see both daughter and son
Who've grown away and flown the nest
Two lonely people, too weary to rest

Two lonely people, with heads held high
They're lonely now, but by and by
Grandbabies come shouting through the door
With love abundant and running o'er

Now young voices in laughter ring
As they play about they shout and sing
These lonely people are not lonely now
As in grateful thanks, before God they bow

Merriel Haworth
September 17, 1970

Jesus Came

My Jesus came to this earth one day
As a tiny baby in a manger He lay
His mission here was to save the lost
He paid the price, what an awful cost

He came to save poor fallen man
And the price He paid was in God's plan
He gave His life on the cross to redeem
The world and to save the lost

He came to Calvary that day
The people jeered along the way
They mocked and scoffed, they pierced His side
He said 'tis finished, bowed His head and died

They built a cross, 'twas made of wood
'Twas rugged and heavy, they made Him bear the load
They beat Him and scourged Him as He climbed the hill
But He had compassion on them still.

Merriel Haworth
Sept. 1970

God's Created Land

The beautiful mountains
Were made by God's hand
Just one of the beauties
In God's created land
The sun, moon and stars
The oceans and the seas
The flowers that bloom
And the birds on the breeze

Merriel Haworth
Oct. 29, 1970

Added Pounds Won't Melt Away

No candy today, no cookies tomorrow
Cause if I eat them 'twill be to my sorrow

For these pounds won't melt and dribble away
If I eat what I oughtn't day after day

Merriel Haworth
Oct. 7, 1971

Reach Out

Reach out to Jesus
He is always there
Reach out in reading His Word
Or in prayer

Reach out in singing
Or clapping your hands
Make a joyful noise
Join angel bands

Merriel Haworth
1970

I Love Jesus

I Love Jesus and He loves me
It makes me feel so happy and free
That He so loved me He came here to be
From His home in glory just to set me free
From sin and shame He paid on Calvary

Merriel Haworth
December 3, 1970

The Bible Says

The Bible says we must live Holy
The Bible says we must be pure
If we would enter heavens portals
We must live a life that's true

The Bible says we must be faithful
The Bible says we must endure
If we would gain that life eternal
We must have a heart that's pure

Merriel Haworth
April 23, 1972

Alice

Sweet little Alice in Wonderland
Your Auntie thinks you're mighty grand

Merriel Haworth
April 25, 1972

No Matter

No matter what other folks do or say
I intend to walk with Jesus all the way

No matter how rough or rugged the road
I know He will lead me; He'll share my load

He makes a way when seems there is none
He leads through the battle till the victory is won

Merriel Haworth
March 5, 1972
Last stanza written
July 9, 1972

Because Of Love
Christ bore my sins on Calvary
He paid the price that set me free
He left His home in heaven above
Gave up His all because of love

Merriel Haworth

Nov. 8, 1972

He Paid The Debt For Me
Jesus paid it all; He paid the debt for me
Yes, Jesus paid it all, and set the captive free
He paid the debt for me that I had owed so long
Yes, Jesus paid it all and filled my heart with song

Merriel Haworth
April 23, 1973

The Closest of Friends

I get do lonely, I get so sad
Where are the friends that I once had?
Where have they gone?
Where are they now?
I guess they have plenty of other friends now

I sit and rock, I rock and cry
Longing for friends from days gone by
But they have their own life, and I'm all-alone
I no longer have friends of my own

I sit here at home day after day
The hairs on my head have all turned to gray
Some loved ones are gone, have been laid to rest
I wonder sometimes if that way is best

Then I think of Jesus, the closest friend I had
And knowing He still loves me makes my heart feel so glad
So I'll trust in Him until He takes me home
And then over there I won't be alone

Merriel Haworth
May 14, 1974

A Change Of Heart
Oh Mighty God, how great Thou art
You've made in me a change of heart
Since I've found you my life has been
Much more complete and free from sin

Merriel Haworth
Sept. 9, 1976

Sunshine
I do believe the sun's gonna shine
When you go your way and I'll go mine

The sun won't shine while we're together
I've had enough of this stormy weather

So you go your way and I'll go mine
We'll give the sun a chance to shine

Merriel Haworth
June 10, 1977

Until Tomorrow
Until tomorrow I'll say goodbye
Until tomorrow I'll try not to cry
Until tomorrow I'll miss you so
Until tomorrow I'll let you go

Merriel Haworth
July 7, 1977

Oh Wonder of Wonders
Oh wonder of wonders
My Jesus loves me
He loved me so much
He died on the tree
To save my poor soul
From death and the grave
He bled and He died
My poor soul to save

Merriel Haworth
October 21, 1977

Talking With God

I love to go to God in prayer
I know He'll meet me there
He brings sweet peace into my soul
A talk with Him will make me whole

I love to have a talk with God
While kneeling there upon the sod
And when I rise, and go my way
His peace goes with me through the day

Merriel Haworth
April 30, 1978

Help Me

Lord help me through today
To do the things I should
Help me to shun all evil
Help me to be good
Help me to be kind and true
To those along the way
Help me to put you first, dear Lord
In all I do or say

Merriel Haworth

Sweet Jesus

Oh Sweet Jesus, how I love Thee day by day
Oh Sweet Jesus, how You've led me all the way
Oh Sweet Jesus, I love Thee more and more
I love Thee, Sweet Jesus, more than ever before

Merriel Haworth
May 1978

Our Healer

He touched me and healed me
I know I am healed
It says in His Word
And His power has revealed

That He is our Healer
Our Savior and Friend
He'll save us from sin
And He'll keep us to the end

Merriel Haworth
Oct-Nov 1978

Alone and Blue

Here I sit alone and blue
So I'll write a letter to the two of you
Wish I could be there, by your side
To take a walk, or take a ride

Or just to sit and talk, or watch TV
Or eat a snack and drink RC
We would have such fun, you two and I
At least I know we sure would try

But you can't come here and I can't go there
We must be content with our bill of fare
Though I love you and you love me
I'll just sit here at home and drink my tea

To my brother and his wife

Merriel Haworth
July 14, 1979

Wonderful Lord

Wonderful, wonderful, wonderful Lord
Jesus, my Savior, is He
Wonderful, wonderful, wonderful Lord
He means so much to me

He comforts me when I am weary
He comforts me when I am sad
He loves me I know
And I love Him so
The best Friend I ever had

Merriel Haworth
May 13, 1980

May God Keep You

May God keep you day by day
As you walk along the way
And keep His love within your heart
From His side don't ever part

Merriel Haworth
Feb. 4, 1979

He Makes A Way

He said He'd make a way for me
When it gets so rough I cannot see

The way that He would lead me on
Until the victory is won

He said He'd take me by the hand
And lead me to the Promised Land

To be forever there with Him
In a world that's free from sin

Written in the Ventura fellowship meeting

Merriel Haworth
July 1980

God Made

God made the sunshine
God made the rain
Sometimes we have sorrow
Sometimes we have pain

But God has promised
We'll be able to bear
Whatever comes to us
If we're humble in prayer

God made the roses
And God made the thorns
And He'll keep us all safely
In His loving arms

Merriel Haworth
November 30, 1980

God Knows

God knows every heartache
And sorrow.
He knows every burden we bear.
He knows and cares for His children.
When we need Him, He's always near.

Merriel Haworth
6-13-1981

He Knows Our Every Sorrow
He knows our every sorrow
He knows our every care
He keeps today and tomorrow
He'll every burden share
He gives me joy and gladness
Deep down in my heart
And when we get to heaven
With Him we'll have a part

Merriel Haworth

Look Up Dear Child
Look up dear child
Just keep your faith in God
Forgetting not to read His holy word
And call on Him
When in your hour of need
The answer will come from the Lord

Merriel Haworth
Aug. 19, 1981

Keep Your Faith
Just keep your faith in God
He is our only refuge
As we travel the path He trod

He will carry us safely over
Our problems here below
And take us home to be with Him
He loves us, oh I know

Merriel Haworth
Sept. 7, 1981

Make Praises Ring

I love Him, I love Him, I love Him, I do
My Savior, my Master, my King
I love Him, I love Him, I love Him, I do
I will make His praises ring

I praise Him for giving His life on the tree
To save this world from sin
I praise him because He included me
And helped me the victory to win

I love You, I love You, I love You, I do
My Savior, my Master, my King
I love You, I love You, I love You, I do
I will make Your praises ring

Merriel Haworth
November 23, 1981

Christ Is The Victory!
Jesus told us so
To the cross He had to go
To redeem us from a world of sin
Satan thought he had us bound
But when Jesus came he found
That through Jesus Christ
We can the victory win

Merriel Haworth
November 30, 1981

Jesus Is The Light
There's a Light at the end of the way
And it's growing brighter every day
As I journey through the darkness
To the light that now I see
I know the Light is Jesus
And He's waiting there for me

Waiting there with arms outstretched
To fold me close into His breast
Saying, come into my arms Dear Child
For here you'll find sweet rest

Merriel Haworth
Feb. 2, 1982

When God Calls Me Home
My Darling I love you
I miss you so much
I desire your kisses
I long for your touch
'Tis always so lonely
Since you have gone
But we'll meet in glory
When God calls me home

Merriel Haworth
February 23, 1982

Hidden Necessities
Take a roll of toilet tissue
Put my feet inside
Pull my skirt down neat around me
The tissue now I hide

Place me in a handy place
Until you tissue's gone
Take from me the hidden roll
You have your needed one

To go with the toilet paper holder she made for the bathroom.
Merriel Haworth
December 30, 1986

Thank You God

I thank You, God for the beauties
Thank You for eyes to behold
Thank you for the hills and mountains
And leaves when they turn to gold

Thank you for the trees and flowers
The red the blue and the green
Thank You for all Thy creation
The beauties that my eyes have seen

Thank You for your love, dear Savior
For Salvation You purchased for me
Thank You for pain You suffered
Because of Your great love for me

Merriel Haworth
Jan. 11, 1987

Waves

Majestic waves came rolling in
Controlled by God's own hand
The beauty of that mighty scene
I viewed from on the sand

I stood amazed at all the force
As waves came rolling in
And thought of all the force behind
The mighty waves of sin

That rage across the universe
On the hearts of sinful men
In need of Christ to guide their steps
And save their souls from sin

Merriel Haworth
Feb. 7, 1987

Let Me Be A Blessing
Let me be a blessing today
To You and someone along the way
Mid the turmoil and the strife
As I go through this life
Let me be a blessing today

Merriel Haworth
Aug. 26, 1987

Year's End
This year is almost over
And the things we can do near done
Till another year is started
And this year's victories are won

What will we do for Jesus
In the New Year just ahead?
We must always try to please Him
And obey the things He said

Merriel Haworth
Dec. 14, 1987

Lonely And Blue
Here I sit
All lonely and blue
So I decided to write
A letter to you

My letter is ready
To go your way
Hope you both have
A very nice day

And many more
Of the same or better
So you'll feel real perky
And write me a letter

I wrote this to send in Jesse and Linda's letter

Merriel Haworth
Nov. 6, 1988

The Answer
Jesus is the answer to your problem
If you only go to Him and pray
Tell Him you love Him and you're sorry
For the wrong you've done along the way

Tell Him that you'll try to do much better
And you'll try His will to obey
Say, only help me now my Lord and Savior
Lead and guide my steps every day

Merriel Haworth
Feb. 4, 1989
My Late Date

I'm outta news
I gotta stop
And into bed
I gotta hop

So bye for now
It's getting late
My bed and me
We gotta date

Merriel Haworth
Sent above poem to Josie in March of 1989

God Bless You

God bless you each and every day
In His own special kind of way
Keep you safe through every hour
In His wonder working power

Merriel Haworth
May 2, 1989

Keep In Touch

Thank you for coming to visit me
I enjoyed it very much
When you can't come for a visit
Please try to keep in touch

Merriel Haworth
June 3, 1989

God Bless And Keep You

God bless and keep you everyday
And keep you safe from harm
Guide your steps along the way
And shelter you in His loving arms

To Aunt Goldie

Merriel Haworth
June 21, 1989

Today's Weather

I'm ready for church
Though it's not quite time
So thought I would write you a cute
Little rhyme

It's hot outside
And this you can be sure
It's so terribly smoggy
The air is not quite pure

Merriel Haworth
June 21, 1989

My Sister

I send my sister roses
Because she is so sweet
And when it comes to sisters
My own just can't be beat

I send them 'cause I love her
And this one thing I know
As the years go onward
My love will grow and grow

To my sister Elsie

Merriel Haworth
July 10, 1989

A Little Bite

I've had my bath
And then my lunch

I'm not hungry now
But I have a hunch

When it's time to eat at church tonight
I'll be ready to have a little bite

Merriel Haworth
October 28, 1989

God Made
God made the birds and the flowers
He made the bugs and the bees
He made the clouds and the sunshine
He also made the trees

He made the hills and the valleys
The mountains all white with snow
The rivers, lakes, and streams
The sky above and the earth down below

Merriel Haworth
January 15, 1990

One Dark Stormy Night
The night was dark and stormy
The wind howled overhead
The lightening flashed the thunder roared
I feared to go to bed

There came a knock upon my door
I fiercely shook with fright
Who would dare to be outside?
On such a dark and stormy night

I slowly crept up to the door
And softly cried, "Who's there?"
No answer came, but I waited still
It seemed no one was there

But all that fell upon my ear
Was only empty air
I cringed and waited, then once more
The rat a tat tat tat tat tat
Came sounding on my door

I peeked out, scared, not knowing what
Might amaze my eyes

It was only that yellow rose bush
That had widely stretched forth its arm
I laughed at myself for silliness
I am safe inside and warm!

Merriel Haworth
May 15, 1990

Fall Chores
The leaves are falling
The grass is growing, too
The leaves need raking
The grass needs mowing
What am I to do?

Merriel Haworth
Oct. 22, 1990

Thank You For My Sister
Thank you Lord, for my sister
I've loved for so many years

Thank you for the love we shared
Through laughter and through tears

We shared so many pleasures
As children growing up together

So many pleasant memories
And each one of them I'll treasure

Merriel Haworth
December 1990

When Life Is Past
Now when this fleeting life is past
And I'm going home at last
Joy and peace await me there
In my blessed Savior's care

Please don't grieve, when I depart
Let there be peace within your heart
I'll be forever safe from harm
To rest secure in Jesus' arms

Merriel Haworth
May 4, 1991

Written for Rue English's family
After she was gone.

The Preacher

There usta be this preacher
He usta be just great
He usta preach it early
And He usta preach it late

He usta get anointed
As the Gospel he did preach
The Saints, they all got happy
The sinners he did reach

These "usta be" good preachers
Is not what our God needs
He needs more "now time" preachers
To glorify His name

Merriel Haworth
April 1992

Seeking Satisfaction

If you're seeking satisfaction
In your life, here as you go
And you seek to fill that emptiness
In a heart that's filled with woe

Just bring that heart to Jesus
Lay it all at Jesus' feet
Let Him fill your heart with joy
Let Him there, all your cares meet

That's the purest satisfaction
When the heart opens up to Him
To empty out all sinful things
And let His love come flooding in

Merriel Haworth
June 28, 1992

Little Prayer

My mind has gone blank
No more news there to find
So I'll close this letter
With a little prayer

God grant peace and comfort
In your heart and home each day
As you yield yourself to him
Let Him have His way

Merriel Haworth
Jan. 1, 1993

Modern Conveniences

My microwave quit waving
And my oven won't bake
My sandwich maker's broken
A sandwich it won't make

My watch won't tell the time
'Til a battery I do get
My clothesline pole lies on the ground
Good thing the clothes aint wet

Though everything is dirty
Aint no need to make no suds
My washer has done cranked out
It wouldn't wash my duds

Merriel Haworth
Jan 10, 1993

Little Bits

Little bits of sunshine
Brighten up the day
Bringing bits of pleasure
To brighten up our way

Little words of greeting
With a smile or two thrown in
Brighten up some other's way
And help us, friends to win
The Best Gift

Had no way to get out
To buy proper gift or card
So I started in to thinking
And thinking very hard

Then I got this brainstorm
Just give what you have on hand
And cause I give with love
I know you'll understand

So I'll just add a line or two
Cause I just want to say
I wish God's very best to you
Mother and Baby Shane

Merriel Haworth
June 7, 1993

To Chuck and Kym
May God bless and keep you, as you journey o're the land
And keep you ever safe in the hollow of His hand

Merriel Haworth
Oct 9, 1993

May God Bless And Keep You
May God bless and keep you
When we're far apart
Just keep His love light shining
Deep within your heart

To keep your footsteps steady
As through life you go
And keep looking upward
He loves you, this I know

Merriel Haworth
November 3, 1993
To end Bonnie's letter

May God Bless and Keep You
May God bless and keep you
Close by His side

And may His love within you
Forevermore abide

Merriel Haworth
November 30, 1993

To Jim and Mary Lou

To Vera and Cecil
May God Bless you day by day
And fill your lives with happiness
All along the way.

Merriel Haworth
Jan 14, 1994

To Mark and Deanna
(Sent With Their Letter)

God loves you very much, you know
Let His love within you grow
It will make life brighter
As you go on spreading sunshine here below

Merriel Haworth
June 13, 1994

The Sins of the World To Pay
He hung on the 'Old Rugged Cross'
In shame and disgrace that day
Gave up His life in great love
For the sins of the world to pay

Merriel Haworth
June 1994

Gratitude For A Job Well Done
Words could never begin to express
The gratitude I feel in my heart
For all the work that was done on my home
To each one who had a part

In bringing such beauty to the home where I live
And giving so much pride
Every time that I view it again
Each time that I step outside

May the blessings of God fill the home of each one
And happiness fill every heart
Of the neighborhood partnership of the city of Montclair
And to each one who has a part

Merriel Haworth
June 1994

Dear Father

Thank you for Your Spirit, dear Father
Abiding with us day by day
Help us to say; Have your way dear Father
In all we do and say

Make me more pleasing to You, Lord
In all I say or do
Mold me and shape me, dear Father
I want to be more like You

Merriel Haworth
Oct. 30, 1994

Bed Early?

Cool again
Heater won't light
If it gets too cool
Bed early tonight

Merriel Haworth
June 2, 1995

TO

To keep my eyes on the Word of God
To walk the path that Jesus Trod

To do the things you would have me to do
To keep my heart forever true

To keep it always pure within
To live a life that's free from sin

Lord, help me live this kind of life
And help me through life's toil and strife

To keep my faith in God above
And bask forever in Your love

Merriel Haworth
Dec. 17, 1994

To My Dear Nephew, Chemey
You were still small when I saw you
But perhaps not today
Since two long years have gone by since then
You are growing up into a strong young man
Remember your Creator in the days of thy youth
And deal always fairly, in honesty and truth
And as you grow older, always follow in His plan
That's what it takes to make the very best man

Love Auntie
Merriel Haworth
April 24, 1995

Happy Birthday
(For Clara Martin and her Husband)

Have a Happy Birthday
Both you and your spouse
And may only happiness
Dwell within your house
As you follow the Savior's leading
And keep your trust in Him
To keep your footsteps steady
And give you peace within

Merriel Haworth
May 10, 1995

Call On Jesus
When you need a helping hand
Call on Jesus
Need someone to understand
Call on Him
If you're burdened down with sin
Call on Jesus
He'll forgive you and take you in
Just call on Him!

Merriel Haworth
October 23, 1995

An Indian's Conception Of The 23rd Psalm

The Great Father above is a Shepherd Chief
I am His and with Him I want not

He throws out to me a rope
And the name of the rope is Love

He draws me and draws me to where the grass is green
And the waters are not dangerous

I eat and lie down satisfied

Sometimes my heart is very weak and faces down
But He lifts me up again into a good road

His name is wonderful

Sometime, it may be very soon, it may be longer
It may be a long, long time
He will draw me into a place between mountains

It is dark there, but I'll draw back not
I'll be afraid not

For it is there between these mountains that the Shepherd Chief
will meet me

And the hunger that I have felt in my heart all through this life
will be satisfied

Sometimes He makes the Love rope into a whip, but afterwards He
gives me a staff to lean on

He spreads a table before me with all kinds of food

He puts His hand upon my head and all the tired is gone

My cup He fills until it runs over
What I tell you is true; I lie not
These roads, which are a way ahead, will stay with me all through
my life

And I will go to live in the 'big tepee' and sit down with the Great
Shepherd forever

Happy Birthday To Betty
(Birthday Nov. 22)

Although you are not my daughter
I'd be happy to own you as such
You are my own sister's daughter
And I love you so very much

You are so kind and so helpful
You're such a blessing to me
A niece like you is so nice to have
You are very precious to me

To Cora Elizabeth (Doran) Wiltse
From your Auntie who loves you
Merriel Haworth
May 11 or 12, 1995

Baby Sister
Dear little, baby sister
Been trying to get you, but then
A little machine stepped forward
And foiled my attempt again

Hope your birthday was happy
My dear sister, Mary Lou
Although it is late, little sister
A happy birthday to you

And Many More!
I Love You!

Merriel Haworth
May 23, 1996

He's The One

Jesus is my inspiration
He's the One
He's the One who guides my footsteps
He's the one I love so much

Merriel Haworth
June 8, 1996

By His Stripes

By His stripes I am healed
By His stripes I am healed
I am saved by the blood He shed for me
When He died upon the tree
Paid the price that set me free
I am saved by the blood He shed for me

Merriel Haworth
June 20, 1996

Blessed Jesus
Thank you, blessed Jesus
For all you are to me
You are my precious Savior
From sin You set me free

Merriel Haworth
Nov. 4, 1996

Mercy
If God showed only justice
For the life we live today
And never showed His mercy
How miserable our state would be!

Merriel Haworth
Dec. 1, 1996

May God Richly Bless You

May God richly bless you
And keep you safe from harm
And may you rest completely
In His loving arms

Merriel Haworth
Feb. 4, 1997

Light

When the lights go out
And it's dark at night
Light this candle and
You'll have a light
To light your way
From room to room
'Til the lights are back on
And I hope real soon

Merriel Haworth
Dec. 17, 1997

A Loyal Friend

When life fall of grief and sorrow
Lies heavily upon my heart
And the dawn of a black tomorrow
Bids tears from my hot, eyelids start
Dear God, if Thou but only
One prayer of mine attend
Leave me not crushed and lonely
Grant me a Loyal Friend!

Merriel Haworth

A Moment With Him

We mutter and sputter
We fume and we spurt

We mumble and grumble
Our feelings get hurt

We can't understand things
Our vision grows dim

When all that we need
Is a moment with Him

Merriel Haworth

A Prayer For The Middle Aged

Lord, Thou knowest better than I
That I am growing older
And will someday be old

Keep me from the fatal habit
Of thinking I must say
Something on every subject
On every occasion

Release me from cramming
To try to straighten out everyone's affairs

Make me thoughtful
But not moody
Helpful, but not bossy
With my vast store of wisdom

It seems a pity nit to use it all
But Thou knowest, Lord
That I want a few friends in the end

Seal my lips on the subject of aches and pains
They are increasing
And the love of relating them
Is becoming sweeter as the years go by

I dare not ask for grace enough to enjoy
The tales of other's pains
But help me to endure them with patience

I dare not ask for improved memory
But give me more humility
And less cocksureness when my memory
Seems to clash with the memories of others

Teach me the glorious lesson that
Occasionally I may be mistaken

Merriel Haworth

An Old Rugged Cross

To a hill far away
Went Jesus one day
To die on an old rugged cross

My sins he did hide
When he suffered and died
Long ago, on that old rugged cross

Merriel Haworth

As To Looks

Some folks in looks take so much pride
They don't think much on what's inside
Well, as for me I know my face
Can ne'er be made a thing of grace

And so I rather think I'll see
How I can fix the inside of me
So folk'll say she looks like sin
But ain't she beautiful within?

Merriel Haworth

Are You?

Are you
Walking now with Jesus
Every hour of every day
All the while with Jesus
Happy on the homeward way

Are you
Planning now with Jesus
Tasks that you may do for Him
Everything for Jesus
Where truth's light is flickering dim

Are you
Pleading now with Jesus
For those souls you want to win
Everyone for Jesus
From their heavy load of sin

Are you
Trusting now in Jesus
That the "work" is almost through
All your faith in Jesus
That His promise will come true

Are you
Looking now for Jesus
To appear up in the sky
Going home with Jesus
Walk and plan with Him on high

Merriel Haworth

Be Loyal To Jesus

Be loyal to Jesus in all that you do
Loyal to Jesus all the day through
He's your Master, your Friend, and your King
Be loyal to Jesus in ev-er-y-thing

Be loyal to Jesus when the storm rages high
Loyal to Jesus when danger is nigh
Be loyal to Jesus all the night through
Be loyal to Jesus; He's loyal to you

Be loyal to Jesus when loved ones depart
Loyal to Jesus, keep Him in your heart
Be loyal to Jesus when loved ones abound
Be loyal to Jesus; He's always around

Merriel Haworth

Beautiful Flowers
We are the children of God
The beautiful flowers of His kingdom
The blossoms that live and grow by His word

Merriel Haworth

Beauty
There's beauty in the fields of corn
There's beauty in the trees
There's beauty in the flowers that bloom
There's beauty in the seas
There's beauty in the hills and rocks
There's beauty in all lands
There's beauty in the prairie, wide
And in the desert sands

Merriel Haworth

Because You Prayed

Because you prayed
God touched our weary bodies with power
And gave us strength for many a trying hour
In which we might have faltered
Had not you, our intercessors
Faithful been, and true

Because you prayed
God touched our eager fingers with His skill
Enabling us to do His blessed will
With scalpel, suture, bandage and better still
He healed the sick, the wounded; and cured the ill

Because you prayed
God touched our lips with coals from the altar fire
Gave Spirit fullness, and did so inspire
That when we spoke sin-blinded souls did see
Sin's chains were broken
And captives were made free

Because you prayed
The 'dwellers in the dark' have found the Light
The glad, good news has banished heathen night
The message of the cross, so long delayed
Has brought them life at last
BECAUSE YOU PRAYED!

Merriel Haworth

Beyond The Cross Roads

Standing at the cross roads
Wondering which way to go
One way seemed so straight and narrow
But beyond I saw a glow

The other was well traveled
It was wide, but dark and drear
And as the throngs went by me
They called, 'come join us here'

Some how I hesitated
I trembled as with a chill
It seemed I sensed a tragedy
For me just over the hill

I turned to the straight and narrow way
And the glow seemed brighter now
In the distance I heard the sweetest singing
It drew me that way, some how

So I started plodding upward
But the way was rugged and steep
I thought I'd never make it alone
So I stopped a while to weep

Then I felt a touch so gentle
Heard a voice so sweet and low
Have faith and trust in me, dear child
I have traveled this way, you know

So now he leads me upward
And each time I stumble and fall
He gently lifts and helps me
He's there when ever I call

The glow in the distance grows brighter
As I travel each step of the way
The singing grows still sweeter and sweeter
He's the Light, the Truth and the Way

The glow in the distance is still brighter
And I hear my Master say
Keep plodding, my child, keep plodding
I'll meet you at the end of the Way

****

Blessed

Jolly May you live
Happy may you be
Blessed with forty kids
Twenty on each knee

Merriel Haworth

Jesus Is The Answer

Jesus is the answer to your problems
If you only go to Him and pray
Lay your burdens there upon the altar
He will walk beside you all the way

Merriel Haworth
February 5, 1989

Behold the Savior

Behold the Savior standing there
With arms outstretched to thee
Inviting you to come to Him
For Salvation, full and free

He bled and died to save you
They drove the nails in His hands

Merriel Haworth

Blessed Brother Urshon

Just keep on keeping on Brother Urshon
And preach the word to people far and near
May people everywhere be blessed as we have
And stirred by the Holy Spirit evermore

I know the Heavenly Father sent you to us
He knows just wheat is needed every time
When we drift out too far He throws the lifeline
And draws us back into His love Devine

The crowds were small but still we love you, brother
For we were fed from God's own Word through you
May God watch o're and keep you ever near Him
And bless you in the work He's given you

God Bless you and your children, ever bless them
For lending you to come so far away
To help our Pastor bring us to the sheepfold
Pray God that none of us will ever stray

Merriel Haworth

Blessed Jesus

Blessed Jesus, He's the One
He will love us 'til the day is done
When the shadows fall around us
His loving arms are still about us
When the trials and tests are come

Merriel Haworth

Chosen Colors

The clear pure white Easter lily
The beautiful, crimson red rose
The crystal blue vase that holds them
Are the colors that I chose

To tell of the pureness of Jesus
And His precious blood that flows
To cover the sins of His people
And wash them white as snow

Merriel Haworth

Brother Coots

Brother Coots came to tell us
Jesus loves and cares for us, too
That He gave His life to save us
He wants us to serve Him daily
And He wants us to love Him, too

Merriel Haworth

By Him Were All Things Made

Life is the breath of God
Breathed into the nostrils of man
Man is but a lump of clay
Shaped by the Master's hand

God is the Spirit of love
By Him were all things made
The sun, the air, the birds that sing
The trees that give us shade

The flowers that bloom in the garden
Their perfume that fills the air
The babies that play around our feet
With locks of curly hair

The sun, the air, the ocean deep
The trees that give us shade
The baby in his crib asleep
By Him were all things made

Merriel Haworth

Come to Him Through Prayer

Jesus is our wondrous Savior
Sent from heaven above
To redeem the poor, lost sinner
Through His endless love

He so loved us that He gave
His life on Calvary
Let them lay Him in the grave
That we might me free

Free from all our worldly sinning
Free from dark despair
Free to choose Him as our Savior
Free to come to Him through prayer

Merriel Haworth

Comfort and Power

He is the King of Kings, 'tis true
Yet He gave His life for me and you
But the grave could not contain
Such love and mercy; such power Devine

So He rose again one day
And before He went away
He said I will send to you
The Holy Ghost to comfort and renew

Merriel Haworth

Coming Home Some Day
When you see my Savior
Tell Him you saw me
When you saw me I was on my way

You may see some old friend
Who will ask you for me
Tell him that I'm coming home some day

Merriel Haworth

Communion With My God
Early in the morning
Before the break of day
I woke up from a night of sleep
And there I knelt to pray

And, Oh I got so happy
In communion with my God
I shouted "Hallelujah"
"Hallelujah, Praise the Lord!"

Rose from my knees with singing
And rejoicing deep down in my soul
I went about my work so lighthearted
My peace and calm restored

Merriel Haworth

Comparing The Gifts

Said the man to the Lord, "See what great things I have given Thee?"
"And now wilt Thou not do some great thing for me?"

Said the Lord to the man, "I gave thee gold;
Thou hast given me copper
I gave thee years, and thou hast given me hours
I gave thee infinite planning
And thou hast given me hasty thoughts
I gave thee a marvelous body
And thou hast given me heedlessness of health
I gave thee a mind of boundless capabilities
And thou hast given me a mind stuffed with trifles
I gave thee love, and thou hast given me indifference
I gave thee many comforts
And thou hast given me complaints
I gave thee prayer, and thou hast given me silence
I gave thee home, and thou hast given me discontentment
I gave thee boundless future, and thou hast given me selfish ambition
I gave thee a world full of men and women
And thou hast given me cold egotism
I gave thee Myself and all of Myself
And thou hast given me only a fragment of thy heart
Tell me, Oh man, what great thing shall I give thee
For all of the great things thou hast given to me?

Then the man said to the Lord, give me only, Oh Lord
Thy forgiveness and thy grace
That I may serve you faithfully all the days of my life
For I am unworthy of the least of thy mercies
And I deserve nothing at thy hands

Yes, Oh yes, how little – how very little – is the most we can give HIM
Compared with what HE has given us!

Merriel Haworth

Dear Sinner

Won't you come to Jesus, dear sinner?
And give your heart to Him
Won't you let His spirit save you?
And cleanse your heart from all your sin
Won't you heed His earnest pleading?
For He's calling you today
Claim you as your Lord and Savior
Let His Spirit fill you all the way

Merriel Haworth

Do You Have Faith?

Do you have faith
To see you through
The daily tasks you set to do

To rise and get to work on time
Polish the car 'til you see it shine

To clean the house; to mow the lawn
These daily tasks go on and on

Merriel Haworth

Do It Now
More than fame and more than money
Is the comment kind and sunny
And the hearty, warm approval of a friend

For it gives to life a savor
And it makes you strong and braver
And it gives you heart and spirit to the end

If he earns your praise – bestow it
If you like him – let him know it
Let the words of true encouragement be said

Do not wait till life is over
And he's underneath the clover
For he cannot read his tombstone when he's DEAD

Merriel Haworth

Don't Be Discouraged
Don't be discouraged when sickness comes
And trials are rolling your way
Don't be discouraged when your mind seems to roam
And temptations lure you to stray
Just look up to heaven and call on our Lord

Don't Cry

Don't you weep
Don't you cry
When it comes my time to die
I am faithful to the test
I'll be with my Lord at rest

Merriel Haworth

Friendly Church

Here's the end of your search
For a real friendly church
On the corner of Linden and Sixth

If you want to find courage
Come and hear Brother Burrage
Be instructed in wisdom and faith

If you're sinking in sin
And need Christ within
There's nothing our God cannot fix

****

Garbage Collector

If I were a garbage collector
And you were yesterday's stew
I'd seize you and elope with you
With you and only you

Merriel Haworth

Fiftieth Birthday

Your 50th birthday is finally here
Don't dread it, but enjoy it my dear
God gave you each moment
Each day and each year
To enjoy and to love Him
And to serve Him while here

Merriel Haworth

For All That You Have Done

Lord, thank You
Because You are my Father

And thank You
Because I am Your son

And thank You, Lord
For ALL that You have done!

Merriel Haworth

Enter In

We'll tell the news to you tonight
If your heart's full of sin
How Jesus came and died for all
To cleanse you from within

We hope you will accept our Christ
Repent and be made clean
And when the gates swing open wide
You each will enter in

Merriel Haworth

For God So Loved The World

For God so loved the world
That He gave His only Son
To die upon the cross
For you and everyone
That whosoever will
May freely come to Him
Believing on His name
And get forgiveness for sin

Merriel Haworth

Get Up And Try Again

If at first you don't succeed
Get up and try again

If at first you don't succeed
Get up and try again
Don't let the devil win
God is able to see you through
Jesus wants you to follow Him

If at first you don't succeed
Get up and try again

Merriel Haworth
✩✩✩✩✩✩

Give Them To Jesus

Heavy hearted
Burdened with care
Load of sorrow
Too much to bear?

Give them to Jesus
He saves from sin
He heals broken spirits
And gives peace within

Merriel Haworth

Get Thee Behind Me Satan

I once was a slave to old Satan
He thought he had conquered my soul
But then I met my Master
Now Jesus has control
I am now living for Jesus
No longer sinking in sin
And when old Satan tempts me
I just say to him

Get thee behind me Satan
I want no dealings with you
You've tried to bar me from heaven
But by God's grace I'll get through
My Savior purchased my pardon
On the cross of Calvary
So get thee behind me Satan
I'm all through dealing with thee

My Savior's coming in glory
He's coming to gather His own
Where He shall reign forever
King of Kings on His golden throne
I long to be with my Savior
And someday I shall be
So get thee behind me Satan
I'm all through dealing with thee

Get thee behind me Satan
I want no dealings with you
You've tried to bar me from heaven
But by God's grace I'll get through
My Savior purchased my pardon
On the cross of Calvary
So get thee behind me Satan

I'm all through dealing with thee

Oh won't you come to my Savior
And give your heart to Him
Let His spirit fill you
And cleanse your soul from sin
Be filled with the Holy Spirit
Baptized in Jesus' name
Then when old Satan tempts you
You can say to him

Get thee behind me Satan
I want no dealings with you
You've tried to bar me from heaven
But by God's grace I'll get through
My Savior purchased my pardon
On the cross of Calvary
So get thee behind me Satan
I'm all through dealing with thee

Merriel Haworth

God Is Our Wonderful Creator

God is our wonderful creator
He created man on Earth and all there in
He so loved the world He created
He gave His Son to die for our sin

Merriel Haworth

God Maketh a Way

God maketh a way
Where it seems there is none
In the darkest of night
When we feel all alone
When temptations beset us
And lure us to sin
He maketh a way
And ushers us in
Into His kingdom
In heaven above
Sheltered and Secure
In His constant love

Merriel Haworth

God Sent His Son
Would you believe such a love as this
Would ever reach mankind
That God so loved the world He sent
His only Son to die

To save a poor, lost world from sin
He sent His only Son
To die upon that cruel cross
Victory over sin and death to be won

Upon that cruel cross of shame
He suffered, bled and died
And He would do it all again
To save folks like you and I

Merriel Haworth

God's Promises

God has not promised
Skies always blue
Nor flower strewn pathways
All our life through

God has not promised
Sun without rain
Joy without sorrow
Nor peace without pain

But god has promised
The strength for the day
Rest from the labor
And light for the way

Grace for the trials
Help from above
Unfailing sympathy
And His undying love

Merriel Haworth

Good Enough

It was good enough for Paul and Silas
Good enough for the Hebrew children, three
It was good enough for Daniel in the lion's den
And it's good enough for me

Merriel Haworth

Guidebook From Heaven

Ask for the guidebook
The Bible from heaven
For our Salvation its pages were given

If for a truth
You are seeking today
Ask for the guidebook, it teaches the way

Thousands are traveling
Death's downward way
Few walk the path that is narrow today

One leads to darkness
The other to light
One is the wrong way, the other is right

Merriel Haworth

Have A Happy Birthday
Have a happy birthday
And many more to come
And may only happiness
Dwell within your home

As you follow the Saviors bidding
And keep your trust in Him
To keep your footsteps steady
And give you peace within

Merriel Haworth

He Is
He is my strength, He is my guide
He's always there, right by my side
To comfort and to guide me
No matter what betide me
He is my strength, He is my guide
He's always there, right by my side

Merriel Haworth

He Cares

I wandered out in the cold, so bold
Alone, in the darkest night
Away form the Master's sheltering fold
So far from His love and His might

I wandered far, in the paths of sin
In darkness I stumbled and fell
Not fearing the danger I was in
On the pathway that leads to hell

But the way grew weary; the night was long
So alone in the cold and the storm
I cried to my Savior to rescue me
Now I'm so safe and so warm

In the shelter of love; in my Savior's arms
Away from sin's dark snares
For He sought me and found me out in the storm
I'm so glad that I know that He cares!

Merriel Haworth

He Knows The Way

Sometimes the way seems rough
And dark and rugged the road
But Jesus is always beside us
To guide and lighten our load

He traveled the road before us
He knows every step of the way
He leads us if we will but trust Him
'Tis ours but to trust and obey

Merriel Haworth

He Lives Again

He was born, a sacrifice to be
On the cross He died for thee
He was born, to save a world from sin
Jesus died; but oh, He lives AGAIN

Jesus lives; He's all in all to me
He bore my sins on cruel Calvary
Gave His life to set sinners free
Again, He lives for you and me

Merriel Haworth

He Liveth Now

To the top of mount Calvary
They led Christ to die
He bore His cross gladly
To redeem you and I
The spear pierced His side
The thorns crowned His brow
He was laid in the tomb
But He liveth now
He's coming in glory
Someday for His own
We'll worship and praise Him
In heaven, 'round His throne

Merriel Haworth

He Will Make A Way

I know not why these trials must come
Into my life this way
I only know I love my Lord
And He will make a way

Merriel Haworth

He Works With Our Young

He works with our young
He's young, too, you know

He works with our young
He's teaching them to work and grow

Merriel Haworth

Help Me

Help me, dear Lord that I may see
The good in everyone

Help me to see in everyone
Only what good is there

Merriel Haworth

Help Yourself to Happiness
Everybody, everywhere
Seeks happiness, it's true.
But finding it and keeping it
Seems difficult to do.

Difficult, because we think
That happiness is found
Only in the places where
Wealth and fame abound.

And so we go on searching
In "palaces of pleasure"
Seeking recognition
And monetary treasure.

Unaware that happiness
Is just a "state of mind"
Within the reach of everyone
Who takes time to be kind.

For in making OTHERS HAPPY
We will be happy, too.
For the happiness you give away…
Returns to "shine on you."

Merriel Haworth

Higher Power

There's a higher power than I
And His home is in the sky
Yet He dwells in the hearts
Of those who on Him will rely
He's the King of kings, 'tis true
Yet He loves both me and you
He gave His life upon the cross
To prove that it's true

He's King of kings, 'tis true
Yet he gave His life for me and you
When He died upon the cross of Calvary
With a heart full of love
He left that blessed home above
And came to Earth and died
To save both you and me

Merriel Haworth

His Mercy

If God would deal with me justly
And give me just what I deserve
He could never show me His mercy
And shower me with His love

But, Oh thank God for His mercy
He forgave me when I repented from my sin
He extended His loving arms to me
And mercifully gathered me in

Merriel Haworth

Holiness Unto The Lord

Praises be to our Lord and King
Praises be to our God
Praises to Him we will shout and sing
Holiness unto our Lord
Holiness unto our Lord
Holiness unto our Lord
Praises to Him we will shout and sing
Holiness unto our God

Merriel Haworth

Holy Spirit, Come
Blessed Holy Spirit come
Make my heart and life your home

Merriel Haworth

Honor Him Everyday, Dear Grandma
The Christ child lay in a manger
So very long ago
The date of His birth, dear grandma
Is something we don't know
So what does it matter, dear grandma
The date that we honor Him
For in our hearts, dear grandma
His promises forever ring
So we honor our Savior today, dear grandma
And tomorrow, forever, and age
And for eons and eons we'll praise Him
God bless you, dear grandma, always

Merriel Haworth

I Began To Pray

I came to Jesus Christ, my Lord
One sad and weary day
I poured my heart out to my Lord
When I began to pray

Merriel Haworth

I Know!

Oh yes I know that He will lead me
Lead me forward to that land

And I know that He is with me
Will be with me to the end

Merriel Haworth

I Know, I Surely Know

I know not what the future holds
As I stand before you, tonight
Holding this little candle
With its flame so pure and bright

I know not if it be smooth or rough
The path that I must trod
But this I know, I surely know
It's all in the hands of God

The strength I need for the way He leads
He gives me every day
No more, no less He knows my needs
I surely know He leads the way
M.H.

****

I Love Thee

I love Thee in life
I'll love Thee in death
And I'll praise Thee
As long as Thou lendeth me breath

And say when the death dew
Lies on my cold brow
If ever I love Thee
My Jesus, 'tis now

Merriel Haworth

I Must Be An Example Of Purity

I must look them in the eyes when I go home
So I am under obligation, as I roam
To be right and clean and square
All the time and everywhere
Or I have to dodge their eyes when I go home

I must look them in the eyes and feel no shame
No conscientiousness of guilt or cause for blame
So, I'll do the best I can
To be every whit a man
Or I couldn't face the folks and feel no shame

I must kiss them with clean lips when I return
So the kisses of the wanton I must spurn
For their sweet belief in me
Un-betrayed it must be
I must kiss with decent lips when I return

I must give what I expect when I go home
Love as wide and high and pure as heaven's dome
Right must triumph in the end
God's own rules we cannot bend
I must give what I expect when I go home

Merriel Haworth

I Will Follow

I was ready to enter the gates of hell
When God reached out a loving hand
Saying; "That's not for you, child of Mine
I'll lead you to a far better land

"Just hold fast My hand and follow My steps
Have faith and trust in My might
I'll lead you to joys that have never been told
I'll lead you through darkness to a bright shinning light"

I turned and I saw He was speaking to me
'Twas to me He was saying; "come home
I love you dear child, I want you for My own
No longer this downward path to roam"

So I turned my steps upward, to follow
And now, with my hand in His own
He leads me through the valleys to high mountaintops
On this journey toward heaven and home

I'll follow wherever He leads, I know
Though darkness assails me and death hovers near
All things work together for good, to His own
He'll never send more than I'm able to bear

He molds me and shapes me through trials and tests
And then when the molding is done
I'll shine like PURE GOLD refined by His hand
Worthy to wear the crown I have won

Merriel Haworth

I Love You, Father
I love You, my Father in Heaven
I love Your sweet, Holy Son
I love You, oh great Holy spirit
I'm glad I can call You my own

Merriel Haworth

I Wish . . .
I wish you happiness; I wish you joy
I wish you first a baby boy

And when his hair begins to curl
I wish you then a baby girl

Merriel Haworth

If The Ocean Were Whiskey

If the ocean were whiskey
And I were a duck

I'd dive to the bottom
And never come up

Merriel Haworth

I'm All Through Dealing With Thee

Get thee be hind me Satan
I want no dealings with you
You've tried to bar me from heaven
But by God's grace I'll get through
My Savior purchased my pardon
On the cross of Calvary
So, get the behind me Satan
I want no dealings with thee

My Saviors coming in His glory
He's coming to gather His own
Where He shall reign forever
King of Kings on His golden throne
I long to be with my Savior
And some day I shall be
So, get thee behind me Satan
I'm all through dealing with thee

Merriel Haworth

I'm Happy

I'm happy
And I don't care who knows

I've Salvation
And I hope that it shows

The Holy Spirit abides
In this heart of mine

I'm Happy
And I don't care who knows

Merriel Haworth

In The Garden Of Eden

In the Garden of Eden
The Bible tells me
Lived a man named Adam
And his wife named Eve
God walked and talked
In communion with them
Until they disobeyed

He planted a tree
That He said don't touch
If you eat of its fruit
You will know too much
'Tis the tree of knowledge
Of good and bad
But they ate of its fruit
Oh, how sad!

Merriel Haworth

Inc 1

All my friends and my relations
Will be waiting there, I know
And my dear, old Daddy
He'll be waiting, too
So I am getting ready brother
Tell me how things are with you
Open wide those pearly gates
I'm coming through

When I look upon my Savior
The one who died for me
And I lay these burdens down
A crown to win
I'll be singing with the angels

******

Ins And Outs

There was a Mama skunk
With two children named In and Out
She had trouble keeping track of them
Because every time In was out, Out was in
One day she sent Out to bring In in
In almost no time Out came in with In
"Out," Mama said, "that was wonderful"
"How did you get In in so quick?"
"There was nothing to it," Out said Instinct!"

****

Ironing Board

I thought and I thought; could I afford
To buy for you an ironing board?
I finally decided, you will discover
To buy for you this pad and cover

Perhaps in the future you will yet
An ironing board somehow manage to get
And then perhaps, if you choose
This pad and cover you can use

Merriel Haworth

Jesus

Blessed Jesus, precious Jesus
Thou art all the world to me
Thou hast purchased my redemption
On the cross of Calvary

Merriel Haworth

Jesus Is Coming

Jesus is coming in glory
I know not the day or hour
But it can't be much longer, my brother
For He has revealed by His power
That the time is so nearly approaching
We haven't much time to wait
Till He shall appear in His splendor
And sweep us through the pearly, white gate

Merriel Haworth

Jesus Is The One Who Died

Jesus is the one who died
To save you from your sin
And His arms are open wide
He'll gladly take you in

If you will give you heart to Jesus
Come to Him today
Yield yourself into His keeping
There is no other way

Listen to His voice, my brother
Cast on Him your cares
Ask Him to forgive your sinning
He'll answer all your prayers

He is waiting for you to answer
Oh, do not delay
Choose Him for your Lord and Master
Just let Him have His way

He'll baptize you with His spirit
For this cause He came
That you might be saved from sin
Baptized in Jesus name

Jesus is the one who died
To save you from your sin
On the cross was crucified
That you might enter in

If you will give your heart to Jesus
Come to Him today
Yield yourself into His keeping
Kneel somewhere and pray

Merriel Haworth

Jesus Loves And Cares For You
Our Brother Coots came to remind us
Of what our Pastor oft' has told
Of the precious story of Jesus
This story will never grow old

How Jesus left heaven and glory
On this old, sinful world to dwell
Just to save our poor soul from destruction
To save us from death and from hell.

Merriel Haworth

Jonah And The Whale

A Bible story I learned when a youth
Is a big fish story, but every word the truth
Just listen right good while I tell you the tale
How Jonah got swallowed by a big fat whale

Now Jonah had sinned and strayed from the fold
Then a big fish caught and swallowed him up whole
There's part of this story but it's awful sad
How the city of Nineveh had gone to the bad

The Lord looked down on their wicked ways
In hopes of repentance in forty more days
The Lord called Jonah and said to speak His word
Go through out the city till every one has heard

If they don't repent of their wicked ways
I'll destroy their city in forty more days
The Lord called Jonah and Jonah said; 'NO!'
'I'm hard shell Baptist, I just can't go.'

'These people of Nineveh mean nothing to me'
'I'm no foreign missionary, and I'll never be'
So he went to Joppa in the greatest of haste
And booked a ship for a different place

The Lord looked down and saw Jonah on board
And old Jonah was just running from the Lord
He set the wind to blowing an awful, awful gale
And the effort of Jonah was beginning to fail

The ship was rocked and tossed by the way
And now Jonah was sorry that he didn't obey
Then Jonah confessed that the storm was caused by his sin
The ship's crew threw him out, but the whale took him in

On the sea's beds the whale tried to rest
He had swallowed his food, but it failed to digest
He got mighty restless and sorely afraid
He rumbled inside while the old prophet prayed

So you see how God's message to Nineveh lays
In the dead letter office three nights and three days
The old prophet shut in as tight as a lock

But things will often open as soon as you knock.

The third day the whale rose up from his bed
Sick at his stomach with pains in his head
And he said to himself, 'I must heave and real quick'
For this old backside is making me sick

As he got to shore he looked all around
Then he vomited old Jonah out on the ground
And he said; 'after three days and nights you have found
That a good man, old fellow, is hard to keep down

He looked all around with a wistful eye
And sat in the sunshine to get his clothes to dry
He thought how much better his preaching would be
From a whale cemetery prophet that's been set free

After he had rested and dried off in the sun
He started off toward Nineveh as fast as he could run
He said I must hurry and also try not to sin
For I sure don't want to be swallowed up again

He arrived at the city about a week late
And preached from the time he entered through the gate
Till the whole population had repented and prayed
And God's hand of vengeance and justice had been stayed

Merriel English

Keep Me Sweet

Lord, keep me sweet when I grow old
And tings in life seem hard to bear
When I feel sad and all alone
And people do not seem to care

Oh keep me sweet and let me look
Beyond the frets that life must hold
To see the grand eternal joys
Yes, keep me sweet in growing old

Merriel Haworth

Lean On Him

Just lean on His eternal arm
He'll give you strength to bear
The sorrow in your heart, today
We know that He doth care

He sees the tear drop in your eye
The sadness in your heart
He knows how hard it is to bear
When loved ones from us part

Merriel Haworth

Left For Me

Here I sit jus pondering the situation
Have lawns to mow
Can't go on vacation
For someone else has gone, you see
'N left the mowing and watering for me

Merriel Haworth

Let Him Lead You

Let Him take your hand and gently
Lead you on from day to day
Sharing al your heavy burdens
As you travel on life's way

He'll forgive you if you ask Him
He will save your soul from sin
Open now your heart to Jesus
Open wide and let Him in

Merriel Haworth

Let Jesus Come In
He will welcome you home
He says to you come
And drink of the water of life
'Tis free for us all
Just answer His call
Let Jesus come into your life

Merriel Haworth

Lifeline
Oh friend
If you're drifting
The dark stream of sin
He's offering the lifeline
Let Him take you in

In faith call upon Him
He'll answer your prayer
Just yield yourself unto Him
You'll be safe in His care

Merriel Haworth

Life's Storms

The wind was blowing fiercely
And the waves were piling high
And all those riding in the ship
Were sure that they would die

But Jesus came walking on the water
He spoke and all was calm
The wind and waves obeyed His voice
He saved them from the storm

If storms of life are vexing you
And there seems no place to hide
Put your trust in Jesus
And in His live abide

Merriel Haworth

Little Sally

Little Sally four or five; had a big sister Jane, not quite two years older than herself. They loved to play together. They played so well together and had so very much fun.

One-day big sister, Jane, didn't want to play. Little Sally was very upset because big sister wouldn't play, so she went off to pout.

Some time later Mother asked; "Where's Sally?"

Jane didn't know. So they searched all through the house; all in vain. They searched the yard, still no Sally. Mother was frightened.

In the backyard was a big hole called a mining shaft; as they lived in a mining community. Mother just knew that her little girl had fallen into that hole.

Jane and Mother asked the neighbors if they had seen Sally. They called Father at work and told him that Sally was missing. He left work to help search for the child

Soon the whole small town was out looking for Sally. . . .

(Sorry Auntie left the story here. I would finish it by finding Sally hiding in the toy box.)

Log Cabin

There's a little, old log cabin
'Neath the trees up on the hill
And beside that old log cabin
That's where my love is waiting still
Waiting there for me to join her
When my life on earth is done
(On that day we'll be together
With God in our heavenly home)

Merriel Haworth

Lord Grant

To save and keep us day by day
Lord grant that You and I
May help to share the load always

To save and keep us from all sin
Lord grant that You and I
May learn to share the load with them

Lord Make Me A Blessing I Pray

Lord make me a blessing, I pray
A blessing to someone as I travel life's way
A blessing to loved ones, or strangers that stray
Lord make me a blessing, I pray

Merriel Haworth

Lord, Thank You!

Lord thank you for keeping me day after day
Thank you for calling and for showing me the way

Thank you for healing and making me whole
Lord, thank you for cleansing and saving my soul

Lord, thank you for giving yourself in my place
Thank you for letting me enter this race

Thank you for strength to meet every test
Thank you for giving my soul peace and rest

Merriel Haworth

Lover Of My Soul

I have my Lord
I Have my Guide
I have my Savior by my side

He dwells within
He has control
He is the Lover of my soul

Merriel Haworth

Make Me Worthy Lord
Oh my Jesus how I love thee
How I long to be with thee
Make me worthy Lord when life is done
To hear thee say well done
Come into rest with me forevermore

Make me worthy Lord
Make me worthy Lord
Worthy to hear you say well done
Make me worthy Lord worthy to enter in
Worthy to hear thee say
Come enter into rest with me, my child

You're welcome home

Merriel Haworth

May You Be Blessed
May you be happy
May you be blessed
In a happy little cottage
With the one you love best

Merriel Haworth

March Forward

Keep plodding, 'tis wiser than sitting aside
And dreaming, and sighing and waiting the tide
In life's early harvest, those only can win
Who daily march forward, and never give in

Merriel Haworth

Mark

Mark is a boy
That gives us such joy
When he's good as good can be

But when he is bad
We are oh so sad
But he'll be good again, you'll see

Merriel Haworth

This sketch was found on the back of a voided check.

Memories

Don't let me forget the crown of thorns
That You wore on Your head that day
The memory of the nail scarred hands
Don't let it fade away

The spear pierced side where blood did flow
To redeem a world from sin
Let me remember, that I may keep
A heart that is pure within

Let me remember the cross You bore
And bear mine each day I live
To Thy glory, dear Lord, that I may help
The message to others give

Merriel Haworth

My Book
Please see Mommy and Daddy
This book is mine
To teach me the Word
Of our Savior Devine
My little eyes can't read it yet
But, oh the pleasure I get
By turning the pages
With loving care
And reading the pictures
That I find there
My God Is Wonderful

My God is wonderful
He made the earth and sky
My God is wonderful
He made both you and I

My God is wonderful
He made the stars that shine
My God is wonderful
Upon the earth, so bright

My God is wonderful
He made the moon and sun
My God is wonderful
To give us light

My God is wonderful

Merriel Haworth

My Lord

I'll go with my Savior
I'll go with my Lord
If I drive a Cadillac
Or if I drive a Ford

If I should have wealth and fame
Or live in a grass hut
My Lord is always with me
The door is never shut

He leads and guides me all the way
And when this life is o're
He'll take me safely through the gate
Where I shall weep no more

Merriel Haworth

My Prayer

Jesus take me as I am
Cast all my fears away
Fill me with Thy Spirit, Lord
Keep me through each day

In the center of Thy will
Help me Lord to do
All the things You bid me, Lord
Help me to be true

Lead me; guide me, Lord, each day
As through life I go
Hoping, trusting in Thy love
More of grace to know

Leading others to Thy throne
By the path You trod
Teaching them to know Thy love
And put their trust in God

And when this life is over, Lord
And in great power You come
May I be ready, Lord, to hear
Thy precious words' "Well done!"

"Come enter into rest My child"
And lay your burden down.
For you a crown of life have won,
A prize of great renown!"

Merriel Haworth

My Sometimes Disposition
Sometimes I'm happy
Sometimes I'm blue
My disposition depends on you

Merriel Haworth
My Tea Party

Nobody likes to stay with me
So I sit alone and drink my tea
They go the way that they fancy
But nobody invites me

They love to go to the mountains
They love to go to the sea
They love to go to the dessert
But I sit alone and drink my tea

They love to go to the river
To fish or swim with glee
They love to have fun at some party
While I'm alone with my tea

Merriel Haworth

No Greater Love
It was just about 2000 years ago
Why He should love me so, I do not know
But, He gave His life for me
As He hung upon a tree
No greater love has no man ever known

Merriel Haworth

No Thumbin' Allowed
You can't thumb your way to heaven
You gotta have your sins forgiven
You can't thumb you way into the Pearly Gates
You gotta make your own decision

Merriel Haworth

Oh Karla, Dear Karla

Oh Karla, dear Karla
We love you so dear
You made our life pleasanter
By your presence here

God has been kind, dear
In lending us you
We know that He loves us
And His love is true

Your smile was so precious
Your voice was so sweet
You cheered everyone
That you happened to meet

Our hearts will be lonely
Now that you're gone away
To add a sweet blossom
To the Master's bouquet

We know not the reason
God took you, my dear
Nor why He saw fit
For us to remain here

But we know that whatever
He doeth is best
So we'll trust in the Lord
And stand firm in this test

Merriel Haworth

Oak Or Nut

When your work seems very hard
And your wages very few
Remember that the great oak
Was once a small nut, too!

Merriel Haworth

Oh Lord

Oh Lord – have mercy on me
I'm a poor, blind sinner
I cannot see
Open mine eyes
To the light of Thy Word
The most precious story
That ever was heard

Merriel Haworth

On A Hill Far Away

On a hill far away
Went Jesus one day
And He carried a cross with Him there

On that cross He hung high
To suffer and die
That we in His kingdom might share

If we only believe
And His spirit receive
He'll come in and abide in our heart

Then He'll live with us there
And remove all our care
He'll invite us to never depart

Merriel Haworth

On Top of Mount Calvary

On top of Mount Calvary
So rugged and high
Went Jesus, my Savior
He went there to die

To save poor, lost sinners
Like you and like me
Yes, Jesus our Savior
He died on the tree

Merriel Haworth

Sung to 'On Top Of Old Smokey

Our Brother Donnie

Donnie, our brother, a birthday?
Another year older, you say?
Why he doesn't seem any older
At least not to us anyway

Not another day younger or older
He always seems just the same
Our brother Donnie don't change
Except that he grows in the grace of our Lord

And he grows even stronger in Him
Through prayer and study of God's Holy Word
And striving others to win
To follow the path way of our Lord

Merriel Haworth

Out Of The Blue

When the sun comes smiling
Through the dark clouds yonder
And the Lord Himself appears
From out the blue

To receive us to Himself
With all the splendor
He has prepared for us forever
For those who have been found true

Merriel Haworth

Pentecostal Message Pentecostal Fire
If Pentecostal messengers would seek and pray
Then they could win some folks most every day
For the gospel that we love so well
Is the message that we love to tell

And when the Pentecostal fire comes down
Folks will know it all around the town
Then we'll throw the devil out the door
And we'll shout the victory forevermore

Merriel Haworth

PEOPLES' PROBLEMS

EVERYONE has problems
In this world of care.

EVERYONE grows weary
With the "cross they have to bear."

EVERYONE is troubled
And "their skies are overcast."

As they try to face the future
While still dwelling in the past . . .

But the people with their problems
Only "listen with one ear"

For people only listen
To the things they want to hear.

And only hear the kinds of things
They are able to believe.

And the ANSWERS that are God's to give,
They're not ready to receive.

So while the PEOPLES' PROBLEMS
Keep growing every day

And man vainly tries to solve them
In his own, self-willful way . . .

God seeks to help and watches,
Waiting, always patiently

To help them solve their problems
Whatever they may be

So may the people of all nations
At last become aware

That God will solve the PEOPLES' PROBLEMS
Through FAITH, and HOPE, and, PRAYER!

Merriel Haworth

Realities

Realities must be faced, my dear
By the husband and by the wife

True, they must love each other
But it takes more to sustain through life

Merriel Haworth

Recipe For Love

- 4 Dozen Kisses
- ½ Cup Teasing
- 1 Cup Squeezes

Method:
Mix the teasing and the squeezing
Then slowly add the kisses
Next mix in the moonlight
And bake in the arms of
A handsome, young man
This is delicious when served properly

Merriel Haworth

Resting

Once my hands were trying
Trying hard to do my best
Now my heart is sweetly trusting
And my soul is all at rest

Once my brain was always planning
And my heart with cares oppressed
Now I trust the Lord to lead me
And my life is all at rest

Once my life was full of effort
Now 'tis full of joy and rest
Since I took His yoke upon me
Jesus gives to me His rest

Merriel Haworth

Revealed

Yes He gave His life to save us
But He lives again today
He came forth that day victorious
When the stone was rolled away

He paid the price for our Salvation
By His stripes we have been healed
And we'll be forever with Him
When His power is revealed

Merriel Haworth

Revival

Roll back your sleeves
Get ready to fight
Revival is coming
It's starting tonight

We'll fight against evil
And fight for the right
Just roll back your sleeves
And join in the fight

Merriel Haworth

Right Where You Are

Right where you are, find work today
Dream not of fields, so far away
He who is faithful, near at hand
He may be called to a foreign land

Work today where you stand
God is the leader; He has planned
His are the rules. The ships are His
He guides His own where treasure is

Ready and true to do His will
Serving Him well, though standing still
Then when He speaks the word to go
You will the voice of duty know

Merriel Haworth

Rose Of Sharon

How it charms me and fills me with gladness
In the beauty and springtime of youth
When I awakened from sin and sadness
And my soul is illumined with truth
But conflicts and trials befall me
When the storms of temptations assail
When the foes of my soul would enthrall me
There's a flower that blooms in the vale

Chorus:
Rose of Sharon, now blooming I see
Rose of Sharon, so precious to me
With my whole heart I sing
Hallelujah! Rose of Sharon, so precious to me

Oh, so many have found this fair flower
And the heart has been cured of its woe
More than all it has virtue and power
Life and healing power to bestow
It's a true source if peace and of pleasure
It's a balm for all sorrow and pain
Should I part with this wonderful treasure
All my life would seem worthless and vain

Chorus:
Rose of Sharon, now blooming I see
Rose of Sharon, so precious to me
With my whole heart I sing
Hallelujah! Rose of Sharon, so precious to me

Sinner hasten to seek this fair flower
E're the garden be shut to the gate
E're the fateful tenable hour
When the angel will say it is too late
For the Rose is transported to heaven
And the Spirit thou grievest away
While the gift of God's beauty is given
Seek that blest 'Rose of Sharon,' today
Chorus:
Rose of Sharon, now blooming I see
Rose of Sharon, so precious to me
With my whole heart I sing
Hallelujah! Rose of Sharon, so precious to me

Rubber Ball Or Bell Of The Ball?

Here I stand so big and round
I'll plant my feet firm on the ground

For if I stumble or if I fall
I'd bounce around like a rubber ball

I'll be so small; I'll look so cute
I'll be fancy in a two-piece suit

Now I'm small; I look so cute
Ain't I fancy in my two-piece suit?

I've shown you one; I've shown you all
Now look at me, I'm the bell of the ball

Merriel Haworth

Safe From The Storm
I wandered out in the cold, so bold
Alone in the darkest night
Away from the Master's sheltering fold
So far from His love and might

I wandered far in the paths of sin
In darkness I stumbled and fell
Not fearing the danger that I was in
On the pathway that leads to hell

But the way grew weary, the night was long
So alone in the cold and storm
I cried to my Savior to rescue me
Now I am so safe and warm

In the shelter of love, in my Saviors arms
Away from sin's dark snare
For He sought and found me out in the storm
I am so glad that He cares

Merriel Haworth

Searching For My Bride

I searched so very, very long
For a girl to be my bride
To walk beside me hand in hand
No matter what betide

My search at long last is at an end
For dear I've found you at last
Will you walk beside me all the way
Until this life is passed?

Merriel Haworth

Since Jesus Made Me Whole

I have a feeling in my soul
Since Jesus came and made me whole
Such love and joy and peace Devine
Just to know that Christ is mine

He came into my heart one day
And washed my sin and guilt away
Now I rejoice and praise the King
For He's my life; my everything!

Merriel Haworth

Sister Imon And Simple Simon
(Or Salvation Full And Free)
Sister Imon met Simple Simon
At the revival there
Said Simple Simon to Sister Imon
Remember me in prayer

Said sister Imon to Simple Simon
That very thing I'll do
Christ died to save us, every one
And that included you

Said Simple Simon to Sister Imon
But, I haven't even a penny
Said Sister Imon to Simple Simon
Sir, you need not any

Said Simple Simon to Sister Imon
You mean Salvation's free?
Said Sister Imon to Simple Simon
'Tis free as free can be
Christ paid the debt for everyone
On the cross of Calvary

Merriel Haworth

Small Gift

You are such a nice person
You just can't resist
To accept this small gift
For I would insist
You accept this small token
Of the love that I feel
But is to seldom spoken
Yet is so very real

Merriel Haworth

So Loving And Kind

Jesus my Savior is loving and kind
So loving and kind is He
He gave up His life on an old rugged cross
To redeem a poor sinner like me

Merriel Haworth

Help me, dear Lord, to keep my feet
Upon the solid ground
Upon the Rock, Christ Jesus
That I may ever stand
Firm and true and always ready
My Savior's will to do
That when He calls I am numbered
Among the chosen few
To be what he would have me be
To go where He would lead
****

Sometime

I'm going to be a Christian
When I have time to spare
But first I must make money
Become a millionaire

I'll give up all for Christ
When I have won great fame
Just now I'm fairly occupied
In trying to make a name

Philanthropist sometime I'll be
And help the sick and low
Today I need more ready cash
To make a social show

Sometime I want to live and give
I'll serve both God and man
Moneymaking fills my hours
I'm working all I can

He made a pile of money
He made a worldly show
He made a plan to freely give
But his summons came to go

Merriel Haworth

Songs For Little Daughter
Wash the dishes little daughter
Pour the water steaming deep
Pile the suds up rich and lasting
Wash the sticky stacky heap

Lift the hands with lively rhythm
Sing a song if it should rain
Rinse the plates with boiling water
Leave them in the rack to drain

Time's a talent; never waste it
Work for God with all your might
But He wants to see those dishes clean
And fresh and smooth and white

Shine the sink and make it sparkle
Germs and ugliness must run
Do it well to make it pleasure
God will say to you, "Well Done!"

Merriel Haworth

Squandered Love

I am so tired, so lonely too
I'm so discouraged and so blue

I left my true love last summer
Thinking I loved only you

I squandered the love
That I once knew

Merriel Haworth

Stand Up For Jesus
Stand up and testify for Jesus
He suffered pain and death for you
He hung upon the cross in shame
His hands and feet driven through
With nails; with thorns they crowned His brow
Oh, won't you stand up for Jesus now?

Merriel Haworth

Start Thinking
Don't you ever think of the bright side of life
Is all you can think of bickering and strife
Of the evil that someone has done to you
Or the bad things that someone might happen to do

Why don't you start thinking of the good that is in men
How Jesus gave His life to save them from sin
Encourage others to think of the good and the true
And see only good in what others do

Merriel Haworth

Strength

We know not what You have in store
But this one thing we ask

That You would give us strength
To meet each coming task

Merriel Haworth

Sunny and Funny

May your life be long and sunny
And your husband be fat and funny

Merriel Haworth

Sunshine And Stars
If the flowers didn't bloom
And the sun didn't shine
And the moon didn't show her face
If the stars didn't glow in heaven above
What would happen to the human race?

God set the sun in heaven above
To make the flowers grow
The moon to give us light in the dark
The stars their happy glow

With out these things to light the dark
And make the flowers bloom
The human race would find itself
All burdened down with gloom

How could we see the Light of the world
Without this earthly part
To give example of God's love
And draw our wondering heart

Merriel Haworth

Table of Blessings

There's a table set before you
Laden down with blessings sweet
The "Bread of Life" is on the menu
Jesus says, "Now come and eat."

And drink the living water
Springing up with joy for all
If we feast upon these blessings
We must answer Jesus call

Merriel Haworth

Take Time To Pray

Have you ever felt discouraged
When things didn't go your way
And thought why should I
Take the time to kneel and pray
I can use my time for other things
And get along just swell
Sure you can, and land in hell
Did you ever take the time to pray
When feeling sad and low
And thank the Heavenly Father
For the things you have below

Merriel Haworth

Auntie's brother

Talk

Help me, dear Lord, from day to day
To hold my tongue secure

To talk about my neighbors less
And talk of Thee much more!

Merriel Haworth

Tempted To Sin

Lord, help me keep my big mouth shut
When other folks begin
To talk about some other's faults
And tempt me too, to sin

Merriel Haworth

Thank You

Thank you, dear Father in heaven
Thank you for this beautiful day
Thank you for the love You have given
And the blessings you send my way

Merriel Haworth

Thank You Note

I thank you one and all
For the lovely gift
I received on Mother's Day
Though I feel so unworthy
Of the honor bestowed on me
But I love my Lord and Master
And every one of you!

Merriel Haworth

Thanksgiving Then And Now

'Twas long ago New England's sun had turned the wheat to gold
So Pilgrim Father's gathered in November's frosted world

And while the white-haired pastor to the silent audience read
Gov. Bradford's proclamation, bent was knee and bowed was head

They were thankful for the shining sheaves that flecked the harvest
field
For God had blessed their labors with a most bountiful yield

And upward through the mighty oaks above the grateful throng
Forward heaven went the chorus of the first Thanksgiving song

The years had borne us outward like a ship crossing the sea
And we have found the harbors of the New World's destiny

To us beneath that banner that has never flared a foe
Come the echoes from the anthems of those Pilgrims from long ago

Age from the proud, historic past that makes us grand
Flits the ever-glorious picture of that faithful little band

Which stood within the sturdy trees deep in that forest, dim
And rendered thanks for gifts bestowed with prayer and sacred
hymn

Our vessels ride the waters with their pennons fair unfurled
And our Navy's are saluted in the harbors of the world

Never dreamed the Pilgrim Fathers in the forest cold and gray
How the seed would grow that they planted on that first
Thanksgiving Day

They were few and we are many; like the oceans golden sand
And our Father holds our future in the hollow of His hand

The granaries of the nation overflow with golden store
And the anthem of Thanksgiving rises high from shore to shore

Merriel Haworth

The Barefoot Boy With Boots On

The night was dark and stormy; the sun was shining bright
The stars were casting burning rays on a storm that raged that night
The lightening struck the cowshed; the cows all chewed their cud
The moonlight set the prairie on fire in the middle of a flood

A barefoot boy with boots on came shuffling down the street
His pants were full of pockets; his boots were full of feet
He was born when just a baby; his Grandma's pride and joy
His only sister was a girl; his brother was a boy

He never was a triplet, but always was a twin
His legs were fastened to his knees, just above the shin
His teeth were fastened in his head, several inches from his shoulder
When he was grown he was a man, and every day got older

One day he married a woman, who quickly became his wife
Her weight was just six hundred; she weighed that all her life
Her head was full of blonde hair; her mouth was full of tongue
They raised a dozen children, all born when very young

The youngest was the baby; the oldest was first born
The good one was the best one; the bad one was the worst
They never knew their ages; they never had to fear
They knew they had a birthday a comin' every year

They never knew their father's age, but always had a hunch
That he was born before the son, the oldest of the bunch
And when they died they could not speak; their names they could not tell
The girls all went to heaven – where the boys went, I won't tell

Merriel Haworth

The Boy In Blue

The office had just opened
When a man quite old in years
Entered in with care worn face
Showing signs of grief and tears
And as the clerk approached him
In trembling voice he did say
I'm waiting for my boy, sir
He's coming home today

Oh, you have made a slight mistake
As you must surely know
This is an express office
And not the town depot
And if your boy is coming home
With smiles, the clerk did say
You'll find him with the passengers
In the station just over the way

Oh you don't understand me
Tremblingly the old man said
He'll not come home with the passengers
But by the express, instead
He's coming home to his mother
With tears the old man said
He's coming home in a casket
My son is coming home dead

Just then a whistle pierced the air
Express train someone cried
The old man rose in a breathless haste
And quickly rushed outside
And from the car a long white casket
Was rolled out on the ground
The scene was most heart-rending
To those who'd gathered 'round

Oh do not handle it rough, boys
It contains my darling Jack
He went away, as you know boys
See how he's coming back
He broke his poor, old mother's heart
Her warning has come true
She said he'd come home dead to us
When he joined the boys in blue

The Broad Way

Which road are you traveling?
Oh friend, please tell
On the highway to heaven
Or the broad way to hell

Bright lights and music
So tempting and gay
Lure them quickly
And drag them away

And I know when life on
This earth is o're
We'll be with our own
Little darling once more

Whatever the trial
Whatever the test
I know that He loves me
And His way is best

The devil will tell them
They don't need to pray
Or study God's Word
Just go the broad way

They'll find the old devil
Is just a big liar
He'll lead them to ruin
And into the fire

Merriel Haworth

Note on original:
Hosea 13:4; No other beside me.
The Cost He Paid

So unworthy here I be
Yet Christ gave His life for me
When He hung upon the cross of Calvary

Thus He paid an awful cost
That the world might not be lost
Oh I praise Him for I know it was for me

Merriel Haworth

The Endless Song

I long for a land where grief is unknown
And pain never causes a tear
Where sunbursts of glory awaken each day
And roses bloom all through the year
A sweet land of beauty, untouched by the frost
Or mildews that rots and destroy
Where friendship endures through ages of time
And life has its fullness of joy

A land where the sunlight is lost in the glow
Of a splendor that eye hast not seen
Where tempests can never distress or annoy
And the heart forgets what has been
But yet, above all I am longing to see
By the gift of His infinite grace
In all the sweet glory of heaven's light
The beauty and joy of His face

Roll onward, glad moments; roll onward and bring
Those visions that time cannot dim
Until with the ransomed we join in the song
That echoes eternity's hymn
To Him who hath loved us and washed us from sin
Our Savior, Redeemer and Friend
To Him who hath loved us, all glory be given
Through ages and years, without end

Merriel Haworth

The Falls

Riding down stream; no effort at all
Just drifting along unaware of the fall
I felt contented; I'm out with the crowd
Doing what they do; oh I was proud

When suddenly the storm clouds seemed hovering near
Somewhere just ahead it seemed I could hear
The roar of the falls, their ever closer now
I must stop, pull aside; someone save me – but how

Now I'm so frightened, though still with the crowd
There's no one to hear me crying aloud
To help from disaster; I'm nearer the falls
Their shrill, laughing voices drown out my calls

Someone help me, oh help me, please help me I plead
My friends are gone now; I'm alone in my need
I must escape from the plight that I'm in
For the stream I've been drifting was the dark stream of sin

There must be someone to help me somewhere
I searched for a friend and I found prayer
I found my Redeemer, my Savior, my guide
He saw my great need; He heard when I cried

Lord save a poor sinner; I cried to Him then
He stretched forth His hand to save me from sin
He's now here beside me; He loves me, I know
He'll lead me and guide me wherever I go

Merriel Haworth

The Handiwork Of Our Lord
The handiwork of our Lord
Is the most beautiful to see
He put beauty in the flowers and grass
He put beauty in the trees
There's beauty in the mountains
Beauty in the hills and plains
Beauty in the hail and sleet
Beauty in the rains
And beauty in the snow
Beauty all around us
Where ever we may go

Merriel Haworth

The Little Boy's Poem
Once a little boy
Was asked to say a poem
But he didn't know one

His Teacher's name was Miss Hodgit
He said:

Here I stand before Miss Hodgit
She may hit me and I may dodge it.

Merriel Haworth

The Long Silence

I dream of her so often
And I watch the mail each day
Feeling that I should get a letter
From Mother Dear, who has gone to stay

My heart aches when I say, "No."
She can't write any more to me
The longing is so great
That I cry so I can't see

My lonely heart cries out in pain
That cuts through me like a sword
I cry out oh why, oh why, oh why
Did she have to go, oh Lord?

Then I pray the Lord for strength
That I may do as well as she
Did in her lovely, happy life
And faithful to Him always be

Merriel Haworth

The Lover Of My Soul
He's the healer of my body
He's the lover of my soul
He's the one who satisfies me
I'm so glad He's in control

When He speaks the winds obey
And the waves will cease to roll
He's the one whom I adore
He's the lover of my soul

Merriel Haworth

The Old Book
'Mother, I've found an old, dusty thing'
'High on the shelf. Just look!'

'Why that's a Bible, Tommy dear;'
'Be careful; that's God's book.'

'God's book!' the wondering child exclaimed
'Then, Mother, before we lose it'

'We better send it back to God'
'You know we'll never use it!'

Merriel Haworth

Once our blessed savior gave His life on Calvary
gave it oh so freely just to set us free
Free from all our earthly sinning
Free from dark despair
To prepare us for His coming
When we'll meet him in the air

For our risen savior will come again some day
And take us to that home above to dwell with Him always
In those mansions
Bright and blessed
Prepared by his own hand
There to be at home forever
In that blessed promised land

Oh the joy that waits us
yonder tongue can never tell
If we only hold out faithful
With our savior we shall dwell

M.H. 1957

Won't you Join Me

I will praise my blessed savior
He has done so much for me
For he pardoned all my sinning
When He died on Calvary

Oh I love Him yes I love Him
For He came and set me free
Free from all the sin that bound me
When He died on Calvary

I am going to that city
Where the streets are paved with gold
Where the flowers bloom forever
And we'll never more grow old

Won't you come and join that number
Of redeemed ones gathering in
When the blessed savior calls us
And we'll all be free from sin

For I know that over yonder
On that day so bright and fair
We will all be glad we entered
For we'll meet our savior there
M.H
1957

A picture that Auntie drew
While she was in school.
Notice her grade.

The One Who Called My Name

I heard a voice from Calvary
It softly called my name
It said come unto me, my child
Bowed down in sin, I came

I found the one who spoke to me
'Twas Jesus Christ my Lord
He took away my burden
And bore the heavy load

He set me free from sin and shame
He cleansed my heart within
He filled me with the Holy Ghost
And now His praise I sing

He'll do the same for you, my friend
If you will heed His call
He'll bear your load of sin and shame
He died to save us all

Merriel Haworth

The Shepherds Voice

I had wandered far away
From the Shepherds fold one day
I was lost and couldn't find my way

Then I heard His voice clear bold
Calling me as in days of old
Safely drawing me back into His fold

Merriel Haworth

The Power Of Silence

Speech, the vehicle of our thoughts to convey
As pigment to painter and sculptor to clay
As stone to the builder, fair temple enriching
Or thread to the weaver in pattern bewitching

God, the Creator, His message proclaims
With planets majestic, eternal in flames
Oh wondrous the chorus through universe ringing
Both angels and men enthralled by such singing

Speech muted and quiet thrills strangely the heart
With thought never uttered, in whole or in part
Men argue and reason, declaim by the hour
When silence would lend far more eloquent power

Merriel Haworth

The Prize
With dimpled cheeks
And laughing eyes
You're a living doll
You win the prize

Merriel Haworth

The Questions Of Life
Where are you tickled each time that you laugh?
Where are you sad when you cry?
How are you living while here on this earth?
You're going where, when you die?

Where are you worried when fear enters in?
Do you really know your creator?
Do you know how He joined all the bones and flesh?
Do you know just what you were made for?

Do you understand the way you are made?

Merriel Haworth

The Rose Of Sharon

I took the rose; its colorings rare
Its beauteous, wax like, texture fair
Brought musings of a better land
As long as I held it in my hand
Yet, from its wondrous, silken heart
It gave its fragrance, but not in part
I crushed it, and there filled the room
An exquisitely, sweet perfume

There was a rose; oh have you heard
Of the Rose of Sharon; Of the Word
The Rose whose fragrance fills the life
Subdues the passions; quells the strife
'Twas crushed; that Rose of wondrous worth
That it might send its fragrance forth
Oh Rose of Sharon, can it be
Thy heart was really crushed for me?

Merriel Haworth

The Skeptic's Daughter

On the banks of Rosedale's water
Where the blooming flowers smile
Lives a pure and lovely daughter
A rich skeptic's only child
Crowned with knowledge, beauty and health
Learned in all her classic attire
She was queen of Rosedale's shore

Famed for genius, sense and wisdom
She became her parents' pride
When she joined the 'Skeptic's System'
She was almost ne'er defied
Far and wide they saw her power
Over all disputants rise
Oh, her genius seems to tower
Like a goddess in the skies

A large meeting was progressing
Near her father's flowery grove
Where the sinners were professing
All the Blessed of Christian love
Father, let me show the bible
To this poor, illiterate clan
That it's nothing but a manual
On the character of man

Go my daughter; you are able
To destroy their Sabbath theme
Go and prove their book a fable
And their doctrine all a dream
Dressed in all her pride and glory
She went forth to join the throng
Where she heard the gospel story
Both in sermon and in song

Soon a thrill of deep conviction
Seized upon her guilty soul
Filled her heart with an affection
That her mind could not control
Calmly rose her, with out falter
And her sins began to tell
So she came before the altar
Where in humble prayer she fell

Casting all her prayer on heaven
All her prayer went to the throne
Till her sins were all forgiven
And the Savior was her own
Then she hastened to her father
To inform him of God's love
And to tell her aged mother
There is a better home above

Well my daughter, it's reported
You have joined the ignorant horde
To their doctrine been converted
All against your father's word
Oh dear mother show me favor
I've not joined the ignorant horde
But I've found the blessed Savior
Who is Christ, our risen Lord

Well my daughter, your behavior
Seals your doom without delay
You must either leave your Savior
Or your father's house today
Oh my father I will love you
Though you drive me from your door
None on earth I'll set before you
But I love my Savior more

Then be gone from me forever
I will see your face no more
All your kindred ties you sever
When you leave your father's door
Only let me have your favor
And I'll be your willing slave
But I cannot yield my Savior
No, I'd rather see my grave

There's your likeness, clothes and purses
Take them and at once depart
For your prayers seem more like curses
To my wounded, broken heart
Goodbye father, will you meet me
Where the happy millions dwell
Here's my hand; oh will you meet me
Where never more we'll say farewell

My dear mother I have often
Thought of riches, pride and wealth
But I'm now an outcast orphan
With no home or friend on earth
Though my father and my mother
Drove me homeless from their door
I've a friend more dear than mother
Who will keep me evermore

Leaving mansions, field and fountain
From this scene she turned away
Up the wild and rocky mountain
Where her path in twilight lay
To the bright and distant sago
Slowly journeyed she along
While her voice in lonely echo
Filled the valley with her song

Rosedale evening mild and gentle
In sweet Zephyr's found the moor
And the night had spread her mantle
As the skeptic left her door
Oh dear Mary, come and listen
To the lovely voice I hear
Oh come quickly now my system
Feels a weight I cannot bear

The wife came out to the veranda
Then she heard the tones abroad
Oh dear husband it's Amanda
In sweet conversation with her God
Hear it through the stormy regions
How its heavenly anthems rise
Oh dear husband her religion
Is the doctrine of the skies

But these words were scarcely spoken
E'er she sank in anguish wild
And the father's heart was broken
As he sped toward his child
Up the mountain dark and lonely
Guided by her heavenly song
Clasped his darling to his bosom
Oh my child forgive my wrong

Oh come home and save your mother
'Tis your prayer that let me live
Come my child, embrace your mother
And our wretched hearts forgive
Oh my parents I'll go to you
And will live the heavenly theme
Singing glory hallelujah
To our Saviors glorious name

Shouting glory to our Savior
She returned in heavenly love
Where her parents soon found favor
In the joys from heaven above
They with all their sins forgiven
Went rejoicing on their way
To their home high up in heaven
In the realms of endless day

Merriel Haworth

The Voice

I heard a voice from Calvary
It softly called my name
It said come unto Me, My child
Bowed down in sin I came

I found the One who spoke to me
'Twas Jesus Christ, my Lord
He took away my burden
And bore my heavy load

He set me free from sin and shame
He cleansed my heart within
He filled me with the Holy Ghost
And now His praise I sing

He'll do the same for you, my friend
If you will heed His call
He'll bear your load of sin and shame
He died to save us all

Merriel Haworth

The Voice Of Jesus Is Calling

Hark, the voice of Jesus calling
Who will go and work today?
Fields are white, the harvest waiting
Who will bear the sheaves away?

Loud and long the Master calleth
Rich rewards He offers thee
Who will answer gladly saying
Here I am, oh Lord, send me

If you cannot cross the ocean
And the heathen lands explore
You will find the heathen nearer
You can help them at your door

Still the voice of Jesus calleth
Few have heard His loving call
Many souls are sadly waiting
He would have us reach them all

Yet we sit and do not answer
The voice that pleads us but to go
Tell the lost ones of Salvation
And the Lord who loves them so

Hark, the voice of Jesus calling
Who will work till day is done?
Still the fields are white with harvest
Will you bring them to the Son?

Merriel Haworth

The Way

I know not what may come tomorrow
But I know that for today
We must follow in His footsteps
Where our Savior led the way

We must follow close beside Him
We must cling unto His hand
'Till we reach that far horizon
Over in the Promised Land

We must tell it unto others
How our Savior led the way
How He gave His life to save them
If they will only choose this way

Leave this sinful world behind them
Rest on Him their every care
He will lighten every burden
He will lessen every heartache
He will every burden share

Merriel Haworth

The Will Of My Master

I want to do the will of my Master
As I travel on life's way
I long to win more souls, much faster
So I must needs watch and pray

Must needs pray and search Thy Scripture
Lest I fail in God's plan
In helping spread the Word to others
Of His love to sinful man

Merriel Haworth

They Were Healed

As they went they were healed
They were healed of afflictions
Great and small
The leper was made clean
The blind were made to see
The deaf were made to hear
The dumb were made to talk
And the lame were made to
Rise up and walk
As they went they were healed
They were healed of afflictions
Great and small

Merriel Haworth

Thrifty New Year's Greeting

For months we have been thrifty
But this month tops them all
We send Season's Greetings
On the paper off the wall

Although it brings good tidings
And our wishes are well meant
We send a New Year's greeting
And it didn't cost a cent

Happy New Year!

Merriel Haworth

Timely Advice

A lineman sat on a telephone pole
Working and smoking away
A small lad's voice, from the ground rang out
Better throw that pipe away
Don't you know it will stunt your growth?

The lineman laughed; but the thought hit its mark
For he tossed away the bowl
If it can't stunt the growth of my physical man
It can stunt the growth of my soul
And my bank account most surely

Merriel Haworth

Timmy

Our Timmy was with us for such a short while
But, Oh how he cheered us with his sweet smile
Then he was taken from us, not by death but by man
I wonder if that was according to God's plan
It seems so unfair for we loved him so
It near broke our hearts when he had to go
He hasn't a Mother, God called her away
And his Daddy's income isn't sufficient to pay
For the keep of five children, so precious and dear
But he has to work, so they were place in the care
Of friends in three homes away from here
But Timmy and the others in our hearts we hold near

Merriel Haworth

Tired and Worn
I didn't take time to pray
E'er I left home this morn
And when it was ended
I came home so tired and worn

Merriel Haworth

To Make This Sinner Free
Thank you Blessed Savior
For all You've done for me
You shed Your precious life's blood
To make this sinner free

Merriel Haworth

Traveling On
Through hills and valleys we travel
Having ups and downs we go

The trials and temptations are many
But there's one thing we surely know

There's a Father in heaven who loves us

Merriel Haworth

True To Laughter
Love to laughter
I'll be true
But not a minute after

Merriel Haworth

Trust

'Tis sweet to trust in Jesus
To know He leads the way
To know he's watching o're us
Lest from the path we stray
He'll keep our feet from slipping
As He walks by our side
And may we ever choose Him
To be our friend and guide

'Tis sweet to feel His presence
So near us every day
Giving us strength from His strength
And teaching us what to say
He'll keep our lips from speaking
The wicked words and sharp
He'll guide our thoughts and actions
And make us pure in heart

'Tis sweet to know He loves us
And bids us come to Him
That he may bless and comfort
And keep us free from sin
And then when life is ended
May we hear the words, "Well Done!"
And receive Devine approval
From the Father and the Son

Merriel Haworth

Trust And Yield To Him

My sister and I have often wondered why
We were left all alone when our mom had to die
For our daddy had gone on to Canaan's fair shore
To dwell with our Savior forevermore

Now our mother has gone on to clasp daddy's hand
And sing glad hosannas in heaven's own band

But our Father in heaven knows best you see
So I'm sure He'll take care of my sister and me
He'll pilot us safely through this world of strife
If we'll only trust Him and yield Him our life

Merriel Haworth

Trust In The Lord
So lonely; so heartsick, discouraged and blue
He'll lift up your heavy load
He'll carry you through
Just hold to His hand
And have faith in His Word
Put not faith in Man, but trust in the Lord

Merriel Haworth

Unchanged
After the Spirit has flown, you see
There's no turning back for you or me
As we are then we shall always be
Unchanged throughout all eternity

Merriel Haworth

Very Near

Jesus is near
So very near
Jesus is near today
Jesus is near
So very near
Just kneel to Him and pray

Merriel Haworth

Virtue

Oh I have touched the hem of the garment
Of the One who died for me
And the virtue left His body
It has set the captive free

And it takes away all pain
If we believe and ask
In Jesus name

Merriel Haworth

Wandering Children

When our children wander far away
From the path where our Savior led
And get themselves in trouble
We know not what lies ahead
But if we keep our trust in God
We know He has control
So we must keep on praying
For God to save their soul

Merriel Haworth

When . . .
When the sun comes smiling
Through the dark clouds yonder
And our Lord appears
From out the shining blue
To receive us to Himself
With all the wonder
He has prepared for all
Who have proven true
That's what I'm waiting for
Aren't you?

When My Life Is Done
When my life on earth is done
And the victory is won
Oh yes, I'm going home to be with God
He loved me so; He came and died
On the cross was crucified
They pierced His side that day
He was crowned with thorns; then laid away
But He rose again one day to set me free
(And I be with Him through eternity)

Merriel Haworth

When A Friend Is Needed

Jesus is near though dark seems the way
And everything seems to go wrong
When loved ones forsake and turn away
He still fills our heart with a song

For His love is dearer than all we have known
He shares every burden we bear
He'll pilot us safely through the darkest storm
When a Friend's needed most, He is there

If we will but trust Him with our hand in His
We can conquer life's darkest storm
Within His arms safely abiding
We will never fear sorrow or harm

Merriel Haworth

When We Get Too Tired To Go To Church
The Devil Laughs

If we get too tired to go to church
The devil's glad
If we get up and go to church anyway
We can make him mad
Then we gain God's smile
And it's so sweet
Satan's left behind when our Lord we meet
Then we feel God's touch and our rest is complete
When we go to church anyway

Merriel Haworth

When You Are Away
It seems like a year
Since I saw you, dear
Though I know it's been only a day
It's so lonely when you are away

Merriel Haworth

When You Are Married

When you are married
And have twins
I'll furnish you with
The safety pins
Merriel Haworth
✶✶✶✶✶✶

Where Ever I May Go

I need no other anchor
With Jesus by my side
He always gives the answer
He'll always be my guide

He is my shield and buckler
My friend against the foe
He'll always walk beside me
Where ever I may go

Merriel Haworth
✶✶✶✶✶✶✶

While God's on His throne

I'm never alone while God's on His throne
His Spirit abides my soul within
He loves me I know; for long ago
He planned to redeem me from sin

He gave His Son; His most Beloved One
To suffer and die there in shame
They scoffed and they scorned
Crowned Him with thorns
And cast lots for His garments that day

Merriel Haworth

Where There Is Love

Where there is love the heart is light
Where there is love the day is bright
Where there is love there is a song
To help when things are going wrong

Where there is love there is a smile
To make things seem all the more worthwhile
Where there is love there is quiet peace
A tranquil place where turmoil's cease ...

Love changes darkness into light
And makes the heart take to 'wingless flight'
Oh blest are they who walk in love ...
They also walk with God above
And when man walks with God again
There shall be peace on earth for all men

Merriel Haworth

If we live in the Spirit, let us also walk in the Spirit; Galatians 5:25
Love does no wrong to a neighbor; therefore love is the fulfillment of the law; Romans 13:1
Where Would I Be?

Where would I be without Him?
I'd be lost out on the sea of life
For I was drifting far away from the shore
In the storm of toil and strife

Merriel Haworth

Which Master?

Which master do you serve?
Which one of the two?
One would drag you off to hell
One died to save you

One laughs at your fall
And would give you a shove
But, the other stoops down to pick you up
In tenderness and love

Merriel Haworth

Why am I Complaining?

My cross is not too heavy,
My road is not too rough,
Because God walks beside me
And to know this is enough . . .

And though I get so lonely
I know I'm not alone
For the Lord God is my Father,
And He loves me as His own . . .

So though I'm tired and weary
And I wish my race were run
God will only terminate it
When my work on earth is done . . .

So let me stop complaining
About my "LOAD of Care"
For God will always lighten it
When it gets too much to bear . . .

And if He doesn't ease my load
He will give me strength to bear it
For God in love and mercy
Is always near to share it.

****

With Our Savior We Shall Dwell

Once our blessed Savior
Gave His life on Calvary
Gave it up oh so very sweetly
Just to set us free

Free from all our earthly sinning
Free from dark despair
To prepare us for His coming
When we meet Him in the air

For our risen Savior
Will come again some day
And take us home above
To dwell with Him always

In those mansions, bright and blessed
Prepared by His own hand
There to be at home forever Yes, Jesus Hears Me
****

(Sung To The Tune For Jesus Loves Me)

Jesus is my all in all
When in need, on Him I call
He will hear and answer prayer
For His power is everywhere

Chorus: Yes, Jesus hears me
Yes, Jesus hears me
Yes, Jesus hears me
He answers when I Call

He will hear you (me) when you (I) pray
He will take your (my) fears away
When in faith on Him you (I) call
Let Him be your (For He is my) all in all

Chorus: Yes, Jesus hears me
Yes, Jesus hears me
Yes, Jesus hears me
He answers when I Call

If your life is filled with sin
If you've doubts and fears within
Cast on Him your every care
He will hear your every prayer

2nd Chorus: Yes He will hear you
Yes He will hear you
Yes He will hear you
He'll answer when you call

Merriel Haworth

Another school picture

In that blessed Promised Land

Oh the joy that awaits us yonder
Tongue can never tell
If we hold out ever faithful
With our Savior we shall dwell

Merriel Haworth

You May Fall

You may fall from the highest mountain
You may fall from the heavens above

But the happiest fall you ever had
Was when you fell in love

Merriel Haworth

Young Love

When I was young and in my prime
I wanted your love; but you didn't mine

But now that you are old and gray
You want my love; but I turn away

For I am still young and I want my fun
But you are much too old to run

I've found a man much younger than you
I love him and he loves me too

So you go your way and I'll go mine
You want my love; but I don't have time

When I was young and love was blind
I loved you; but you were unkind

I've found a new love, don't you see
For you are much too old for me

Merriel Haworth

Your Family Of Three
Sitting in Young People's Service, tonight
I remembered I had forgotten to write
To our dear little sister, Mary Helen Hughes
Who's been acquiring some cute little baby shoes
And little garments that hold such charms
When worn by the boy she now holds in her arms
With this sweet little babe in her home, I'm sure
There will be many changes, but what is more
He'll bring many joys, contentment and mirth
As he grows and develops and plays around the hearth
To his mother and daddy none else can compare
Until there's a brother or sister there
May God watch over your family of three
Guide and protect you all until eternity
Then stretch His arms and enfold you in Love
When he takes you to dwell in bright mansions, above

Merriel Haworth

Your Fate
Your fate is in your hands
It can go higher or lower
As your appetite demands
If you would see pounds and ounces roll
Of your appetite YOU must control

Merriel Haworth

Your Hour
This is your hour
Time waits for no man
Accept Him just now
For that is His plan
God's Spirit will not always
Strive for your soul
Accept Him just now
And make heaven your goal

Merriel Haworth

Auntie's words of wisdom

Hanging On To Something?
Take this whole world and give me Jesus
Do we really mean what we say?

Of course we want Jesus with all of our heart
But can we let all else slip away?

Or are there some things we MUST hang on to?

Merriel Haworth
March 1959

Soul Winning And Personal Work

Dos and Don'ts

Dos:

- Do – learn the scripture, enough to speak with authority
- Do – ask questions encouraging a person to speak out of his heart
- Do – pray for wisdom, posses Brother Love rather than Brother know-it-all
- Do – be a good listener
- Do – be enthusiastic
- Do – avoid long stories

Don'ts

- Don't – argue, but reason together
- Don't – preach or lecture, but witness
- Don't – boast in ourselves
- Don't – point the finger in anyone's face
- Don't – run down the other people's church
- Don't – pick green fruit
- Don't – force, beg or coax

Scripture References:

Proverbs 11:20
Psalms 126:6
Matthew 4:19

Merriel Haworth
April 11, 1961

Lambs Of God

Little lambs of God
Come and hear me say
You must reach that point of contact
Before you stray away

Merriel Haworth
March 11, 1962

Auntie's Casserole

1 lb ground round, browned
3 potatoes
2 onions
Garlic
Bell pepper
1 pkg frozen peas
Cheese
Salt
Pepper

Tomato juice

Thank You
Words could never begin to express
The gratitude I feel in my heart
For all of the work that was done on my home.
To each one who had a part
In bringing such beauty to the home
where I live'
And in giving me so much pride
Every time that I view it again,
Each time I step outside;
Thank you.

May the Blessings of God fill the homes of each one,
and may happiness fill each heart of the Neighborhood Partnership
of the city of Montclair.
To each one who had a part, again, thank you.

June 1994 – M. H.

A picture done in school---notice the grade...

Cover Picture

Bees

I wish to let loose swarm of bees that will make Honey for you in your Christian Experience. Keep them on the go ALL the time.

- *Bee – Forgiving in spirit*
- *Bee – Strong in the Lord*
- *Bee – Strong in Faith*
- *Bee – Over comers Through Christ*
- *Bee – Of good cheer*
- *Bee – Tenderhearted toward others*
- *Bee – Doers of the Word of God*
- *Bee – Open to instruction*
- *Bee – Slow to condemn*
- *Bee – Dead to yourself*
- *Bee – Much alive in Christ*
- *Bee – Slow to anger*
- *Bee – On the altar of God*
- *Bee – In a prayerful spirit*
- *Bee – At prayer meeting*
- *Bee – Quick to testify*
- *Bee – Ready to serve*

Merriel Haworth

Brother Bowler And The Tulip

Lady said, "I' a tulip"
Brother Bowler said, "A What?"
She said, "a tulip,"
"When I die I want to be planted by a tree."
"So I can come back as something alive."
Brother bowler said, "I'm Born Again"
She said, "You're what?"
He said, "I'm "born of God."
"When I die I'm going to Heaven to be with Him."
She said, "That sounds even better than being a tulip."

Merriel Haworth

Brush Arbor Preaching

Someone gets saved – goes down
And pours out booze in the river
Someone gets up and sings
Shall we gather at the river
~*~
What Brother Bowler told
When teaching Sunday School class
Said we had a great time back in those days.

Merriel Haworth
August 4, 1985

Sound Advice

An old church elder who attended church <u>regularly</u>, but at times caused a heap of <u>trouble</u> for the congregation, told his Pastor that <u>he</u> <u>would</u> soon visit the Holy Land.

"And <u>when</u> <u>I</u> get there," he said with glee, "<u>I'll</u> <u>climb</u> to the top of Mount Sinai and <u>I'll</u> read the Ten Commandments."

"<u>I</u> <u>can</u> tell you something better to do," <u>said</u> <u>his</u> Pastor, "stay home and keep them."

~*~

<u>It's</u> wonderful to know the Bible; it's more <u>wonderful</u> to do what it says!

This was on a Sunday School offering envelope I found. The words underlined were fill ins where the envelope was torn off.

Aunties favorite poems by others

Jesus Set Me Free
I was in sin's prison
When Jesus said to me
I have signed your pardon

You may now go free
Then the tears rolled down my cheeks
The loveliest words I could hear
For when I was in sin's prison
It seemed like many a year

I've heard it told many a time
That Jesus was never there
But I'd rather believe my own eyes
For I know it was He that was there

Bonnie English
Feb 1975v

Our Ancestors

Our ancestors were monkeys
By critics we are told
They contradict the Bible
And knock it's teaching cold

Although the Bible tells us
In Ecclesiastes one
The things already past
Again are to be done

Lady monkey has no worry
About covering up her form
She doesn't even worry
About clothes to keep her warm

While the ladies of our day
Are either wearing fur
Or heading back again
Where the critics say they were

And they all have us guessing
As we see their naked knees
Will they go back where Darwin
Had them all climbing trees?

H. C. English
237 E Maple St
Ontario, CA.

The City Of Jasper

Once I was alone and bowed down with sin
But Jesus found me and he took me in
And He made me a promise that I was His own
And in His kingdom He would give me a home

And I'll sit by the river 'neath the life giving tree
And enjoy all God's wonders that my eyes can see
For I know I'll have access, by God I am told
To that City of Jasper with streets of pure gold

I cried, show me the way; and the Savior replied
I am the way; it was for you I died
It was for me He suffered death's awful sting
So I'll shout Hallelujah, and His praises I'll sing

And I'll sit by the river 'neath the life giving tree
And enjoy all God's wonders that my eyes can see
For I know I'll have access, by God I am told
To that City of Jasper with streets of pure gold

I'll bathe in the waters that flow from God's throne
And I'll walk in the valleys, but never alone
And I'll shout Hallelujah, while the angels all sing
For I'll dwell in the presence of Jesus, my king

And I'll sit by the river 'neath the life giving tree
And enjoy all God's wonders that my eyes can see
For I know I'll have access, by God I am told
To that City of Jasper with streets of pure gold

Show us the way, a lost world did cry
And to show us the way, God's Son had to die
He showed us the path the ransomed must trod
And it leads to that City whose builder is God

And I'll sit by the river 'neath the life giving tree
And enjoy all God's wonders that my eyes can see
For I know I'll have access, by God I am told
To that City of Jasper with streets of pure gold

The day is soon coming when the wicked shall fall
To the rocks and the mountains, to hide the they'll call
But the blessed are ye, God's commandments who hold
For ye shall have access to that City of Gold

And I'll sit by the river 'neath the life giving tree
And enjoy all God's wonders that my eyes can see
For I know I'll have access, by God I am told
To that City of Jasper with streets of pure gold
James E. English

The Rose, The Gopher And Faith

I watched a rose, a beautiful rose
Turn toward the sun and die
And as I watched its head hang down
A tear dropped from my eye

And then I saw, as I hung my head
The answer was clear as day
A gopher caused this rose to die
And its beauty to fade away

And I thought as I gazed at the rose
My life is just the same
And it to was faded and torn
For I'd lost touch with Jesus name

Now listen and I'll tell you
How faith no longer grows
But fades and withers and dies at last
Like the gopher and the rose

James E. English
****

Worship On Our Knees
(Sung To 'On Top Of Old Smokey')

Place your hand on the Bible
And state e'er I die
That you'll meet me in Glory
In that home built on high

We'll meet by the river
And shout 'neath the trees
And we'll fall down and worship
Our King on our knees

Jimmie

Written on calendar page for
October 19, 1946

What Doth The LORD Require?
Micah 6:6-8

How shall I come in the presence
Of the ruler of Heaven and Earth
In what way I do approach Him
I, of lowly birth
He is so high and exalted
Yet, He has taken the trouble
To notice a sinner like me

Then what can I do to approach Him
Can I make an offering, sweet
Of the things of wealth I've collected
And lay such things at His feet
Are these the things I should bring Him
And go along in my way
Forgetting to thank and to praise Him
For blessings He gives me each day

No, this is not what He has shown me
The things that would gladden His heart
It is Love, Joy and Peace I must search for
And never let them depart
For with these in my heart I can conquer
The evil and sin of this earth
His Spirit is with me and in me
To help me be of some worth

So Lord, give me Love for my brother
And Lord, make me wise unto Thee
That I through Your infinite mercy
Can help some lost sinner see
That Your Love reaches out to all people
Inviting ALL to come in
And receive for them self the great richness
Of Pardon And Grace for their sin

Jesse Lee English
May 31, 1969
Corvallis, OR

Where Are All The Members?

How often I think, as I sit in Church
And look at the empty pews
"Lord, where are all the people now
That should be here worshiping You?"

Are they ill, too ill to come out today?
And give praise to Your holy name
I pray that You touch them as when You were here
And healed the sick and the lame

Perhaps they're weary from a long week's work
And stayed at home, thinking it best
But didn't You say, 'Child come unto Me
When weary, and I'll give you rest?'

Oh Lord, are they absent just from neglect
Preferring to go their own way?
It may be they're needing another touch
Of Your love in their lives today

Oh Lord, may Your Spirit enter anew
Into hearts that are lonely and sad
Kindle a fire in their soul, Oh Lord
To make them alive and glad

And then when the time for worship comes
And I enter Your House of Praise
I'll be surrounded with love to You
For Your unsearchable ways

Jesse Lee English
May 10, 1976

Getting Late
It's getting late
The day's been long
Though every thing is fine
Though chatting's been a lot of fun
It's time to draw the _____

Jesse Lee English

My Wish For You

What do I wish for you, my friend
As along through life you go
Do I wish you wealth that you do not need
And fancy things to show

Do I wish you a name among the great
As greatness is known today
That other men as they pass you by
Would tribute to you pay

These are not my wish for you, my friend
'Nor are they a wish for me
I would wish for you contentment and health
And Christian liberty

That your needs are supplied from day to day
By Him who supplies each need
That your faith may be strong in Him
That you know you are His, indeed

So that when the King says to me, "Well done,
Your troubles and trials are through."
That the same words are spoken to you, my friend
This is my wish for you!

Jesse Lee English

Our Best

Would you love to give a bouquet to someone
But you just can't afford the flowers?
I'll tell you a 'secret,' just spread good cheer
In this wonderful land of ours

A word of praise for a job well done
Or comfort to one who is sad
Or even a smile to a passerby
May make a faint heart glad

A cup of water, the Master said
To one who has thirsty grown
Is like a man who has done his work
And very good seed has sown

So scatter the petals both near and far
With scarcely a pause for rest
For there is never a cause for a sad regret
To those who have done their best

Jesse Lee English

- 324 -

What Is A Birthday

What is a birthday, Mother dear?
I'd like you to stop and ponder
Is it just a day, like all the rest
Or something special, I wonder

I'd like to consider, Mother dear
Our life as a charted station
With sign posts along the way
To guide our destination

Three score and ten years, Mother dear
The wise man might be given
We can't reverse, or start over again
We only are forward driven

They may be happy years, Mother of mine
Or they may be sad and weary
The choice we make as we go along
So let's keep them bright and cheery

For we choose the pattern, Mother of mine
That makes our life worth living
Or else we have chosen the other kind
And all has seemed un-for-giving

So Happy Birthday, Mother dear
For this one, and every other
So that when we have reached the end of the race
There'll be no regrets to bother

Jesse Lee English

Dear Daughters of the King;

Jesus Christ made you part of His great plan when He purchased your Salvation and brought you an eternal Thanksgiving Day. This wonderful experience and relationship with Christ will last until the veil is lifted and we see Him face to face.

To a born-again, Spirit-filled Child of God today is our Thanksgiving – for indeed, "this is the day which the Lord hath made; we will rejoice and be glad in it." Psalms 118:24

Josephine English

Recipe for A Happy New Year

Take twelve fine, full-grown months. See that these are thoroughly free from old memories of bitterness, rancor, hate and jealousy. Cleanse them from every clinging spite. Pick off all specks of pettiness and littleness; in short, see these months are freed from all the past. Have them as fresh and clean as when they came from the great storehouse of time.

Cut these months into 30 or 31 equal parts. This batch will keep for just one year. Do not attempt to make up the whole batch at one time (so many persons spoil the entire lot this way) but prepare one day at a time as follows

Into each day put 12 parts of faith, 11 parts of patience, 10 parts of courage, 9 parts of work, (some people omit this ingredient and so spoil the flavor of the rest), 8 parts of hope, 7 parts of fidelity, 6 parts of liberality, 5 parts of kindness, 4 parts of rest (leaving this part out is like leaving the oil out of the salad – don't do it), 3 parts of selected resolutions. If you have no conscientious scruples, put in about a teaspoon of good spirits, a dash of fun, a pinch of folly, a sprinkling of play and a heaping cup full of good humor.

Pour into the whole – Love, and mix with vim and vigor. Cook thoroughly in a fervent heat, garnish with a few smiles and a sprig of joy. Serve with quietness, unselfishness, and cheerfulness; and a Happy New Year is a <u>certainty</u>.

Josephine English

Doris Naomi English

Doris Naomi, twenty-seven months old daughter of H.C. and Effie English, passed away at a.m. January 6th, 1929. Funeral conducted by H.J. Murphy, and was laid to rest in the cemetery at Cleveland, Tenn. There to remains until our God shall come again and place her in our arms. She shall come again to her own border with her six little brothers and sisters that have gone on before.

The night of the ninth it rained hard and these words came to me:

> Now the rain is falling fast
> O'er my baby's grave;
> Oh, how long will sorrow last
> Ere my God shall save?
>
> Ere my spirit flies away
> To my unchanging God,
> Ere I hear my savior say,
> Thy path hath well been trod
>
> So child, tonight, look above
> And lean upon His breast,
> His heart is full, yes, full of love
> And thou shalt find sweet rest
>
> There my Lord with outstretched arms
> Will press me to His heart
> Free from all these awful storms
> Where babe and me won't part
>
> And we will sound our voices loud
> Till they hear them in the skies
> Where we will never wear a shroud
> Or see a mortal die

H.C. English

And our family wants to express our thanks and appreciation to the many friends for their help, and sympathy in this hour of trial and grief.

Life For Us

I've been a worker most my life
I've done things cruel to man
I'm try now to live my life
In a way that's meant for mine
God gave us love and gave us breath
He gave us all we need
He gave us life and gave us death
And power to bear a seed
To have a man or have a wife
A child from God's own heart
To live with them throughout your life
A beautiful place to start
So live for God all your life in everything you do
And you will keep all your life he's got a place for you

Mark English

Happy Days

Remembrance is a golden chain
Death tries to break, but all in vein
To have, to love and then to part
Is the greatest sorrow of one's heart

The years may wipe out many things
But this they wipe out never
The memory of the happy days
When we were all together

Effie English

Willie's Speech
I am just a little fellow
And I can't say very much
My speech is this
I am glad I am a boy
I had rather be a boy than a girl or anything
Boys have good times
They can swim and skate and coast
Ride horseback, climb trees, slide down banisters
And most girls can't
I wouldn't be a girl
NO, not if you gave me the best jackknife in the world

Given by Uncle Bill in grade school
William David English

www.ingramcontent.com/pod-product-compliance
Lightning Source LLC
Chambersburg PA
CBHW031234090426
42742CB00007B/193